An Introduction for Adult Helpers

As a teacher and a science education consultant, I have developed many hands-on science experiments. This book is a collection of my most successful science activities, which I have demonstrated hundreds of times, either in my classroom or at my consulting sites.

The activities in *Showy Science* are clustered around scientific concepts and principles that are closely related to elementary and junior high school science curricula. It is an excellent supplementary hands-on activity guide that can make science lessons fun and meaningful. Additionally, the principles taught have application to other common life activities. For example, simple siphon activities can lead to making a bean-sprout-growing device and self-watering devices for house plants.

Ordinary household objects are the major resource for these activities. Even a simple science apparatus costs some money, and many teachers, parents, and students are reluctant to buy an apparatus to conduct just one scientific investigation. Ordinary objects such as pop bottles and jars are economical, abundant, and easy to handle.

Even though this is an activity guide for elementary and intermediate grades, lay people will find it interesting. Various activities such as different methods of propagating house plants and building self-refilling bird baths are intriguing solutions to everyday problems. My ultimate goal was to present science in a fun and interesting way.

Hy Kim

Teachers, Parents, and Other Adult Helpers,
please take note:

Some of the activities in this book involve matches, hot plates, hot water, scissors, or other sharp tools. Below are the symbols used to alert you to any safety issues:

Flame used

Heat used

Chemicals used

Safety needed

In the activities involving these safety issues, I've included notes to students, directing them to seek adult help. The results of these activities can be quite "showy" and safe, too, with your help and guidance.

An Introduction for Students

The activities in *Showy Science* cover a variety of science topics, allowing you to explore the air, water, earth, and animals around you, as well as forces that act upon you. You can do many of the activities alone or with adult help, but a great number of them will be more fun if you demonstrate them for your family, friends, or classmates.

Each activity includes:

- a list of things you will need to perform the activity
- illustrations to help you as you work
- the reasons behind the results of each activity
- information and terms to help you expand your scientific knowledge

Note that some experiments involve matches, hot plates, hot water, scissors, and sharp tools. Below are the symbols used in the book to alert you to any safety issues for an activity:

 **Flame used**

 **Heat used**

 **Chemicals used**

Safety needed

If you conduct an activity that includes one of the above symbols, ask an adult to help you do it safely. If the experimental result doesn't turn out as described, try to find out what factors might be causing it to not work. By trying again and again until you figure it out, you can learn the science concepts better and understand how to control the variables. You may find many fascinating ideas to investigate with simple materials as well as gain excellent science fair project ideas.

Have fun with the many scientific investigations in this book.

Hy Kim

From *Showy Science* published by GoodYear Books. Copyright ©1994 by Hy Kim.

Quick

SHOWY SCIENCE

EXCITING HANDS-ON ACTIVITIES

That Explore the World Around Us

HY KIM

Youngstown State University

Illustrated by Harvey Hirsh and Rebecca Hershey

GoodYearBooks
An Imprint of ScottForesman
A Division of HarperCollinsPublishers

Acknowledgments

Unless otherwise acknowledged, all photos are the property of ScottForesman.

61: Richard Huchings/Photo Edit   **85:** Superstock   **107:** E.R.
Degginger/ANIMALS/ANIMALS   **113:** E.R. Degginger/ANIMALS/ANIMALS
228: NASA

GoodYearBooks
are available for most basic curriculum subjects plus many enrichment areas. For more
GoodYearBooks, contact your local bookseller or educational dealer. For a complete catalog
with information about other GoodYearBooks, please write:

GoodYearBooks
ScottForesman
1900 East Lake Avenue
Glenview, IL 60025

Designed by Elizabeth A. Thompson.
Copyright © 1994 Hy Kim.
All Rights Reserved.
Printed in the United States of America.

ISBN 0-673-36091-1

    5 6 7 8 9-MH-01 00 99 98 97

CONTENTS

Activities for Exploring Air

The Standing and Collapsing Balloon	2
Inflating the Balloon Inside the Bottle	3
The Dancing Penny	4
A Penny Dancing Contest	5
Which Bottle Produces a Greater Number of Dances?	6
A Balloon That Refuses to Go Into a Bottle	7
The Reluctant Balloon Becomes Obedient	9
A Magic Way to Drop the Balloon Into the Bottle	10
How Can You Take the Ballon Out of the Bottle?	11
Demonstrating a Partial Vacuum	13
A Strange Way to Lift a Canning Jar	15
Mason Jar Hocus Pocus	16
Crushing Pop Cans	18
A Spectacular Water Spout	19
A Pop Bottle Thermometer	21
The Water Shooting Contest	23
A Homemade Barometer	24
The Simplest Homemade Barometer	26
How to Make an Altimeter	27
A Tornado Machine	28
The Breathing Lung Model	31

Breathing Plants   34

A Collection of Oxygen Bubbles   36

A Spectacular Fire Flame   37

Rusting Steel Wool   38

Does a Solid Expand When Heated?   40

A Great Bet!   42

A Balloon-Ball Stunt   43

Blow the Balloon Out of the Funnel Easily!   45

The Hovering Balloon   46

The Atomizer   48

Spinning Soda Cans   49

A Pop Bottle Whistle   50

A Pop Bottle Musical Instrument   51

A Cupped-Hands Whistle   52

Whistling Sounds by a Whirling Bottle   53

A Model Ear   54

A Hot–Air Balloon   57

Activities for Exploring Water

The Water Trick   62

A Self-Refilling Water Bowl for Pets   63

Water Jets I   65

Water Jets II   67

A Series of Provoking Tasks   69

The Obedient Diver   70

How Many Paper Clips Can a Cup Hold?   72

A Water Dropping Contest   73

Floating Pins, Needles, and Paper Clips   75

Sink the Paper Clip   76

The Floating and Sinking Egg   78

A Straw Hydrometer   79

Floating and Sinking Soft Drinks   81

How Much Sugar Is in a Can of Soft Drink?   82

Why Does Warm Water Float and Cold Water Sink?   83

A Water Hourglass   86

An Automatic Smoking Machine   87

Climbing Water   89

A Cotton Wick Siphon and Water Clock   91

Climbing Color Bands   92

Analyzing the Pigments in Green Leaves and Flowers   94

Growing Large Salt Crystals   96

Ice Power   98

Ice Cream Shake-Up   99

Ice Puzzle   100

Picking Up an Ice Cube With a Toothpick   101

Activities for Exploring Animals

A Pop Bottle Aquarium   **104**

Small Animals in the Pond Water   **106**

A Snail Aquarium   **108**

Duckweed Farm   **109**

A Demonstration of Eutrophication   **111**

An Aquarium for Mosquito Fish   **112**

Fish and Green Plants   **114**

How Does Cold Water Affect Fish?   **115**

Separating the Babies   **116**

Growing a Monarch Butterfly   **116**

Mosquito Aquarium   **119**

Mealworm Farm   **123**

Peeling an Eggshell   **126**

Disappearing Chalk Pieces   **127**

The Swelling and Shrinking Egg   **129**

Activities for Exploring Plants

A Self-Watering Bottle Planter   **132**

How Does a Bean Change Into a Bean Plant?   **135**

Sprouting Corn Seeds   **137**

What Is Phototropism?   **139**

A Bag Greenhouse   **140**

What Is Geotropism?   **141**

What Is Thigmotropism?   **142**

Sprouting Questions — 143

Does Talking to a Plant Affect Its Growth? — 145

In a Planter, Do Many Plants Do as Well as One Plant? — 146

Growing Bean Sprouts — 147

A Plant Self-Watering System — 149

An Auto-Watering System for Potted Plants — 150

Growing Plant Cuttings — 152

Growing a New Geranium From a Old Geranium — 154

A Water Evaporation Contest — 156

Growing an African Violet From a Leaf Cutting — 157

Growing a Peperomia Plant From a Leaf Cutting — 158

Growing Rex Begonia From a Leaf Cutting — 160

Growing a Spider Plant From an Offset — 161

Growing Plants From a Potato and a Sweet Potato — 162

Does a Sprouting Potato Need Fresh Air? — 165

What Is Hydroponics? — 166

Growing New Plants From Bulbs — 167

Activities for Exploring Microbes

Rotting Banana Slices With Yeast — 170

A Bottle of Carbon Dioxide Gas — 171

Does Yeast Grow Better in a Warm Place or a Cold Place? — 176

Does Yeast Grow Without Food? — 178

Does Yeast Grow Better in a Dry Place or a Moist Place? — 179

Does Yeast Grow Better in a Sunny Place or a Shady Place? — 180

From Sugar to Alcohol — 181

Growing Bread Molds — 185

Looking Into Bread Molds — 187

Growing Bread Mold From Spores   **189**

Growing Blue-Green Molds   **190**

How Quickly Do Bacteria Grow?   **192**

The Germ Theory of Disease and Our Defense Systems   **194**

How Does the Salting of Food Prevent Microbes From
Spoiling Food?   **196**

Microbes in the Community   **198**

Activities for Exploring Gravity, Motion, and Other Forces

Guess Which One Falls First!   **200**

Which Ball Will Strike the Floor First?   **202**

Finding the Center of Gravity of a Piece of Cardboard   **203**

Balancing on a Pencil Point   **205**

Balancing a Ruler   **206**

Standing an Apple on a Toothpick   **207**

A Pendulum   **208**

An Aerodynamic Pendulum   **210**

An Aerodynamic Pendulum String   **211**

How Does the Foucault Pendulum Work?   **212**

A Marble Game   **213**

A Gravity-Powered Race Car   **216**

Magic Tricks   **218**

Seat Belts and Flying Drivers   **219**

The Rolling Coffee Can   **222**

A Pop Bottle Rocket   **224**

Count Down, Blast Off!   **227**

The Water Engine   **229**

The Cloud Machine   **230**

A Balloon Rocket   **231**

Will Water Spill From an Upside-Down Cup?   **233**

The Moon's Orbit of Earth   **234**

The Phases of the Moon   **236**

What Force Keeps the Moon From Flying Away?   **237**

A Propeller-Powered Helicopter   **239**

A Paper Helicopter   **241**

A Paper Airplane   **242**

Square Puzzles   **244**

Clay Boat: Challenging Problems   **246**

    How Do You Measure the Volume of a Lump of Clay?   **246**

    Why Is the Clay Lighter in Water Than in Air?   **248**

    Can You Make the Lump of Clay Float?   **250**

    Loading Cargo in the Boat   **251**

    How Many Marbles Can a Cup Hold

        on the Surface of Water?   **251**

A Penny Barge   **252**

Activities for Exploring Earth

Day and Night   **256**

Clockwise or Counterclockwise?   **257**

What Makes Seasons?   **259**

Is the Earth Closer to the Sun in Summer or Winter?   **262**

A Latitude Finder   **264**

The Length of Day and Night   **266**

What Causes Wind?   **269**

Land Breezes and Sea Breezes   **271**

A Wind Vane   **273**

A Pinwheel   **274**

Activities for Exploring Light

A Poster Board Saw 278

Color Blending With the Spinning Wheel 280

More Color Blending 281

Color Illusion 282

Rolling Reader 283

Do We Really See the Sun Before It Rises and After It Sets? 286

A Rainbow on Your Ceiling 288

Why Is the Sky Blue? 290

Why Is the Sun Red When It Rises and Sets? 291

Funny Faces by Mirrors 292

A Money-Making Machine 294

Polygons and Angles With Mirrors 297

Mirror-Image Puzzles 299

A Periscope 301

Index 303
Annotated Bibliography 307

ACTIVITIES FOR
EXPLORING

AIR

The Standing and Collapsing Balloon

Cap a bottle with a balloon. If you place the bottle in a container, the balloon will inflate and stand up. If you place the bottle in a different container, the inflated balloon will shrink and collapse. Nothing comes in or goes out of the bottle, but the balloon still grows and shrinks.

For this activity, you need:

○ a round balloon

○ a two-liter pop bottle (or a glass juice bottle with a small mouth)

○ a bucket (or dishpan) of cold water

○ a bucket (or dishpan) of warm water

To do this activity:

Place the mouth of the balloon over the opening of the bottle as in the illustration. Place the bottle in the bucket of warm water, and splash the water over the bottle. If you have an audience, ask them what they think will happen to the balloon. Keep watching!

The balloon will begin to swell as the air inside the bottle gets warmer. It may even pop off the bottle! If this occurs, remove the bottle from the warm water, and put the bottle into the cool water for a while. Replace the balloon, and place the bottle into the warm water again.

After the balloon inflates, remove the bottle from the warm water and place it in the cool water. Again, watch what happens. The air inside the bottle will cool, and the balloon will collapse. Repeat the activity to make the balloon inflate and collapse as many times as you want.

From *Showy Science* published by GoodYearBooks. Copyright ©1994 by Hy Kim.

Why does this happen?

When you cap the bottle with a balloon, some air is trapped inside. When you place the bottle in warm water, the bottle and the air inside it warm up. Air is made up of many tiny particles called *molecules*. These air molecules move slowly when the temperature is cold. They move quickly when the temperature is warm. The faster molecules hit the walls harder and more often. This raises the pressure and pushes out the walls of the balloon.

Therefore, when you put the bottle in warm water, the expanded air pushes against the sides of the balloon and inflates it. When you put the bottle in cold water, the air molecules slow down, reducing the pressure, and the air takes up less space. As the air contracts, the balloon collapses.

Inflating the Balloon Inside the Bottle

Would you be amazed to see a balloon taken into a bottle and inflated inside? It is easy to demonstrate.

For this activity, you need:

○ the same materials you used for the previous activity, "The Standing and Collapsing Balloon"

To do this activity:

Do not cap the bottle. Place the uncapped bottle in hot water to warm the air inside it. Ask someone from the audience to assist you by holding the bottle in the hot water while you cap the balloon on the bottle's mouth.

Remove the bottle from the hot water and put it in cold water. Splash the cold water over the bottle to cool the air inside. Watch what happens.

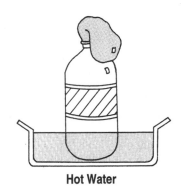

Hot Water

Cold Water

The balloon will be pulled inside the bottle. When this begins to happen, stretch the balloon a little to help it go into the bottle more easily. The balloon will now inflate.

Why does this happen?

You warmed up the air in the bottle by putting it in hot water. This caused the air in the bottle to expand. Some of the air moved out of the bottle. You trapped the remaining air in the bottle by capping it with the balloon. You then put the bottle in cold water. This caused the air in the bottle to contract, drawing in the balloon. Higher pressure air from the outside inflated it.

The Dancing Penny

A penny on the mouth of a pop bottle can dance all by itself if you arrange the bottle in a special way. The penny will be lifted up and dropped again and again.

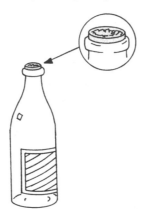

For this activity, you need:

○ a pop bottle
○ a freezer
○ a penny
○ water

To do this activity:

Before you perform this feat, place the pop bottle in the freezer for a few minutes. If you have an audience, announce that a penny will dance on a bottle by your command. Sprinkle a few drops of water on the penny. Take the bottle out of the freezer, and place it on a table. Put the penny on the bottle's mouth with the wet side down. Say a magical word like "Abracadabra!" Soon the penny will rise and fall repeatedly, as if it is dancing.

Why does this happen?

When you took the bottle out of the freezer, the air contracted inside the bottle. When you placed the bottle on the table, the air inside was warmed by the room temperature. The warm air expanded, broke the water seal, and pushed the penny up. As a result, the penny rose and then fell by its own weight as expanded air lifted it. The cycle repeats until the temperatures and inside and outside air pressures are equal.

A Penny Dancing Contest

A variation of the previous experiment can be a fun and exciting party contest.

For this activity, you need:

○ an identical bottle and penny for each person or group
○ water

To do this activity:

Before the contest begins, give the participants a demonstration. This time, do not place the bottle in the freezer first. Place a wet penny on the mouth of a bottle.

Hold the bottle and watch the penny. The penny will rise and fall.

Why does this happen?

Your body temperature is higher than room temperature. Therefore, the heat from your hand will warm the bottle and the air inside it. The heated air expands and pushes the penny up.

Now for the contest! Ask the participants to do the same activity and to explain why the penny dances. After everybody practices the experiment once, announce that half the participants will watch the other half do the experiment. The first half will count and record how many times the penny dances. Switch places so everyone has a chance to try the experiment. Compare records. The person who makes the penny dance the most times is the winner. Discuss the difference among records even though the bottles and pennies were the same for everyone.

Which Bottle Produces a Greater Number of Dances?

Ask the participants to predict which bottle among several odd-sized ones will produce the most penny dances. As they conduct the experiment to investigate their predictions, discuss why one bottle may produce a greater number of dances than another.

For this activity, you need:

- ○ several different sizes of bottles
- ○ an equal number of pennies
- ○ water

From *Showy Science* published by GoodYearBooks. Copyright ©1994 by Hy Kim.

To do this activity:

Keep all the bottles at room temperature. Have each person choose a bottle with which to experiment. Instruct him or her to place a wet penny on the mouth of the bottle. Tell them to warm the bottle by holding it. Count the number of penny dances.

Why does this happen?

If the temperature is equal among all the bottles, then the number of dances depends on the capacity of each bottle. If the bottle has a very large capacity, the number of penny dances will be greater than for a small capacity bottle.

A Balloon That Refuses to Go Into a Bottle

In this activity, you will place a water balloon on an empty jar (see the illustration). You will then ask someone to push the balloon into the jar. It looks easy, doesn't it? To everybody's surprise, no one will be able to push the balloon into the bottle!

For this activity, you need:

○ a balloon
○ water
○ a bottle (a half-gallon orange juice bottle works well for this activity)

To do this activity:

Fill the balloon with water by covering the end of a water faucet with the opening of the balloon. Turn the water on slowly until the balloon is larger than the mouth of the bottle. Tie the neck of the balloon. Dip the balloon in water, and then place the balloon on the mouth of the bottle. Ask a volunteer to push the balloon into the bottle without breaking it. The volunteer may not use any other material to complete this task except his or her own body.

As the volunteer tries to push the balloon into the bottle, a force will keep pushing it back!

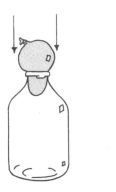 

When the volunteer stops trying to push the balloon, the balloon will return to its starting position. Invite another volunteer to try, or try it yourself!

Why does this happen?

It is difficult to push the balloon into the bottle because the air inside the bottle is trapped by the balloon. Pressing the balloon into the bottle compresses the air inside the bottle. Air takes up space. You push the balloon in; the compressed air pushes it out. When you stop pushing in, the air inside is still pushing out and it pushes the balloon out to its starting position. At that time, the air is no longer compressed and no longer moves the balloon.

The Reluctant Balloon Becomes Obedient

You can push the balloon into the bottle easily, if you know how to tame the reluctant balloon!

For this activity, you need:

○ the supplies from the last activity
○ a drinking straw

To do this activity:

Place a drinking straw in the mouth of the bottle. Wet the mouth of the bottle (this helps the balloon slide in more easily). Fill the balloon with water as you did before, and dip it in water. Place the water-filled balloon on the mouth of the bottle.

Press the balloon into the bottle with one hand while holding the straw in the other. The balloon will slide down into the bottle with very little force.

Why does this happen?

When you press the balloon into the bottle, the trapped air escapes through the straw. This eliminates the air pressure that pushes against the balloon.

A Magic Way to Drop the Balloon Into the Bottle

This demonstration looks like pure magic! You will use a simple scientific principle to drop a water-filled balloon into a bottle.

For this activity, you need:

- ○ an adult helper
- ○ the materials from the last activity
- ○ a piece of tissue paper
- ○ a match
- ○ a pencil or stick

To do this activity:

Crumple a piece of tissue paper and stuff it into the mouth of the bottle. Ask your adult helper to light it with a match. As it burns, push it to the bottom of the bottle with a stick or a pencil.

Dip a tied, water-filled balloon in water. Place the balloon onto the mouth of the bottle. Watch what happens. You may be able to see the balloon dance as it releases air bubbles from the bottle. Then the balloon will be pulled into the bottom of the bottle.

From *Showy Science* published by GoodYearBooks. Copyright ©1994 by Hy Kim.

Why does this happen?

The flame inside the bottle heats the air, making it expand. The expanded air escapes from the bottle through the air bubbles between the balloon and mouth of the bottle. Soon the flame goes out because the burning uses up the oxygen. As a result, the heated air cools, shrinking its volume and creating a lower pressure. The higher air pressure outside the bottle then pushes the balloon into the bottle.

How Can You Take the Balloon Out of the Bottle?

Taking the balloon out of the bottle is not an easy task.

For this activity, you need:

○ the materials from the last activity

To do this activity:

Hold the bottle upside-down with the balloon inside. Grab the balloon's neck, and position it in the center of the bottle's opening. Now, while holding on to the balloon, turn the bottle upright.

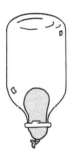 

If you have an audience, ask them what they think will happen when you pull on the balloon. To everybody's surprise, the balloon will stick in the bottle.

As you pull on the balloon, the bottle will lift with it. The balloon does not just slide out. Pull the balloon up carefully so that the balloon does not break. Release your grasp, and the balloon will snap back into the bottle!

Ask your audience for ideas to complete this task. One suggestion might be to heat the bottle. This will expand the air inside the bottle and push out the balloon. That is a terrific suggestion because it works! However, an even simpler solution to this dilemma is to place a drinking straw between the balloon and the mouth of the bottle, as in the illustration. This allows you to pull the balloon out easily.

Why does this work?

When you attempted to pull the balloon out of the bottle, the air inside the bottle grew thinner as the trapped space grew larger. A completely empty space is called a *vacuum*. In this experiment, a partial vacuum formed inside the bottle.
This is evidence of a basic scientific law. Powerful atmospheric pressure constantly presses down on the earth. This pressure comes from enormous layers of air above the earth. In the experiment, you can see this atmospheric pressure in action as it pushes on the bottle and balloon. When you tried to lift the balloon, you were attempting to lift the weight of most of the air over the balloon. You will be able to demonstrate many things by using atmospheric air pressure in the following activities.

From *Showy Science* published by GoodYearBooks. Copyright ©1994 by Hy Kim.

Demonstrating a Partial Vacuum

Because we live on the bottom of an ocean of air, a large air pressure acts upon us. It does some mysterious things around us, too. If a vacuum or low air pressure spot exists, the air pressure around it pushes on it forcefully. You can demonstrate the power of air pressure by creating a partial vacuum.

For this activity, you need:

- ○ an adult helper
- ○ clay
- ○ a plastic container with a smooth bottom
- ○ birthday candles
- ○ water
- ○ a match
- ○ a rubber canning ring (optional)

To do this activity:

Place some clay in the middle of the smooth bottom of a plastic container. Set two or three candles upright in the clay. Add water to the container, submerging the clay. Ask an adult to assist you in lighting the candles.

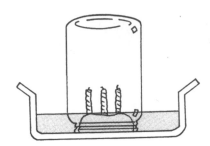

Place the bottle over the flame of the candles. Rest the rim of the bottle on the bottom of the container. Watch what happens. The flames will slowly go out because of the lack of oxygen. Try to lift the bottle straight up. The whole system will rise instead of just the bottle. The container is powerfully attached to the bottle.

If the bottle and container are not smooth, water will seep into the bottle instead of creating a tight seal. This seal is needed for the success of this activity. If you need a better seal, place a rubber ring between the rim of the bottle and the bottom of the container.

Why does this happen?

The covered flames go out because the oxygen in the trapped air is used up. The fire warms the trapped air, causing it to expand and push air out of the bottle. When the fire goes out, the hot air cools. This cooling causes the air to contract, thereby creating a partial vacuum in the bottle. The atmospheric pressure forces the bottle and container together. This is why the whole system lifted while you were trying to lift only the bottle.

A Strange Way to Lift a Canning Jar

This is a good problem to liven up a class or a party. Challenge people in your audience to lift a canning jar by a string attached to the lid. The lid is not secured to the jar. After the participants try without success, show them that you can lift the jar by the string.

For this activity, you need:

○ a canning jar with a lid and ring (not a one-piece cap)

○ transparent tape

○ about 20 centimeters of string

○ hot water

To do this activity:

Tape one end of the string to the middle of the lid. Discard the ring. Your task is to lift the jar by holding only the string. You are not allowed to use the ring. Let each participant try to do it in his or her own way.

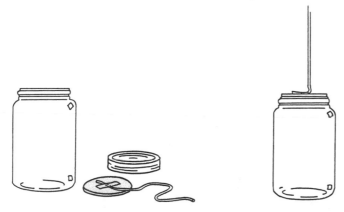

To do this, first submerge only the jar in hot water for about 30 seconds. Next, remove the jar from the water. Empty any water from the jar. Put the lid on the jar and hold it firmly for a while. This will securely seal the lid to the jar during this cooling-down process. While you are waiting, listen carefully for the sound of air leaking out from the lid or jar. If you do not hear a leaking sound, lift the string and move the jar around. The jar and lid will be tightly attached. If you do detect a leaking sound while waiting for the jar to cool, repeat the process of heating the jar and replacing the lid. Wet the lid and press down on it for a while. After the jar cools, lift the string.

Why does this happen?

The hot jar warmed the air inside it. The air expanded, and some of it left the jar. When the jar cooled, the air inside also cooled and contracted. The lid stopped the air's movement from outside to inside the jar. This formed a partial vacuum. The greater air pressure outside the jar pushed the lid and jar together.

Mason Jar Hocus Pocus

This activity is good for a magic demonstration. You can create a partial vacuum in a mason jar that will seal the lid to the jar so powerfully that nobody can pull it off!

For this activity, you need:

- ○ an adult helper
- ○ a piece of paper tissue
- ○ a match
- ○ a mason jar with a rubber washer
  (take off the wire device that presses the cap on the bottle)
- ○ a pencil or stick

To do this activity:

Crumple a piece of paper tissue and stuff it into the mouth of the jar. Ask the adult to light the match and set the tissue on fire.

From *Showy Science* published by GoodYearBooks. Copyright ©1994 by Hy Kim.

While the flame is burning, push the tissue to the bottom of the jar with a pencil. Put the lid on the jar. As the flame goes out, lightly press the lid as you say, "Abracadabra! Alika Zam! Hocus Pocus a la Peanut Butter Sandwiches!" Ask anyone to pull off the lid from the jar. No one can do it!

How can you get the lid off of the jar? One easy way is by pulling the small handle of the rubber washer. As the corner of the rubber washer slides out from the rim, air can enter the jar. As the air pressure equalizes between the inside and outside of the jar, the lid can be easily removed.

Rubber Washer →
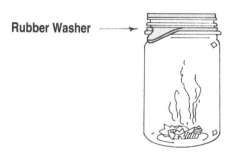

Why does this work?

The lid cannot be removed because of the partial vacuum concept demonstrated earlier when you dropped a water balloon into a bottle.

Crushing Pop Cans

This is an eye-catching demonstration.

For this activity, you need:

○ an adult helper
○ a few empty aluminum pop cans
○ a hot plate
○ a container of water
○ kitchen tongs

To do this activity:

Have an adult heat an electric hot plate or other heating device. Put a teaspoonful of water into an empty aluminum can. Heat it until the water boils.

Using kitchen tongs or an oven mitt, quickly remove the can, flip it over, and push the open side down in cold water.

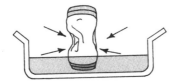

"Pop" and "crush"! (Sometimes, the can will suck in water instead of being crushed if the air or water in the can is not hot enough or if you handle the can too slowly.)

From *Showy Science* published by GoodYearBooks. Copyright ©1994 by Hy Kim.

Why does this happen?

As it is heated, water changes into a gas which takes up more volume and pushes air out of the can. When the can is placed in the cold water, the gases in the can cool off very quickly. Some of the water vapor changes into water, shrinking its volume. As that happens, the can either draws in water or air pressure crushes it. This is another example of the partial vacuum concept.

A Spectacular Water Spout

In this activity, you can make a spectacular water spout touch down on your table just like a tornado.

For this activity, you need:

○ a flask with a rubber stopper to fit its mouth
○ glass tubing
○ a hot plate or other heat source
○ a jar
○ a piece of cardboard
○ water

To do this activity:

Cut out a hole in the center of the cardboard large enough to fit the mouth of the flask. Insert the tubing through the stopper. Fill the jar with enough warm water so the end of the tubing will be submerged when the flask is suspended over the jar.

Pour a half-cup of water into the flask. Insert the stopper and tubing into the mouth of the flask. Have an adult help you boil the water on a hot plate as shown above.

When the water is boiling, turn off the hot plate and remove the flask with kitchen tongs or oven mitts. Hold it upside down, placing the mouth of the flask through the cardboard hole. Watch what happens. A spectacular water spout will surge up violently like a tornado.

Why does this work?

The hot, expanded air in the flask cooled when you removed it from the hot plate. As a result, the water was forced into the flask. Moisture in the hot air began to condense as the air cooled, creating low pressure. The water spout reached maximum speed as the cooling accelerated the system. This forced the water from the jar into the flask. Once the flask was filled with water, the spout stopped.

From *Showy Science* published by GoodYearBooks. Copyright ©1994 by Hy Kim.

A Pop Bottle Thermometer

This activity results in a homemade pop bottle thermometer that shoots water. Your thermometer will show you that air is not the only thing that expands and contracts. Water and other liquids expand as they are heated and contract as they are cooled. By using this principle, you can make a water thermometer.

For this activity, you need:

○ an adult helper
○ a glass pop bottle with a plastic cap
○ scissors
○ a clear drinking straw or glass tubing
○ rubber cement
○ cold water
○ food coloring

To do this activity:

Ask an adult to help you twist the point of your scissors into the middle of the plastic bottle cap. Make a hole big enough for the drinking straw. Insert the straw and seal it to the cap with rubber cement.

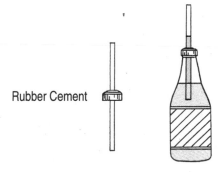

Rubber Cement

Fill the pop bottle with cold water until it reaches the level of the cap when placed on the bottle.

Add food coloring to the water so you can easily see the water's movement through the straw. With the straw inserted, tighten the cap on the bottle. Hold the bottle for a while. Your hands will heat the bottle and the water and air inside it. The resulting increase in volume of water and air will push water up through the straw. You will see the water column move upward and eventually shoot from the straw.

For a similar activity, you need:

○ an adult helper
○ two pop bottles with plastic caps
○ scissors
○ cold and hot water
○ two straws
○ rubber cement
○ food coloring

To do this activity:

Make holes in the caps, as in the last activity. Insert a straw into each cap, and seal with rubber cement. Now, fill one pop bottle with cold water until the water reaches the top. Fill the other bottle only slightly above the bottom of the straw. Add food coloring to each bottle. Cap each bottle tightly. Heat both bottles by placing them in a container of hot water.

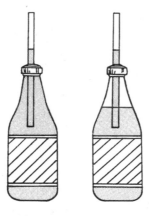

What happens in these activities?

In which of the bottle thermometers does the water move more quickly? Why? From this experiment, you will see that the water moves more quickly in the bottle with less water. The water column in the other bottle will move at a slower pace. This shows that air also expands by heat.

A thermometer that accurately registers temperature uses the same principle. Commercial thermometers do not use water; they use ether alcohol with red color, mercury, or a metal coil. Alcohol is not as expensive as mercury, nor does it freeze as easily as water does. If thermometers used water, the water's volume would increase at the freezing point, breaking the thermometer.

From *Showy Science* published by GoodYearBooks. Copyright ©1994 by Hy Kim.

The Water Shooting Contest

This is a fun science activity for a class or party. The contestant who shoots the water from the bottle thermometer first wins. Each contestant can use his or her own ideas on how to warm the bottle.

For this activity, you need:

○ several pop bottle thermometers as described in the previous activity

To do this activity:

Fill the bottles with cold water. Screw on the caps with the straws inserted and sealed. The water level in each bottle should be about equal.

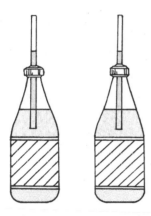

Divide the contestants into small groups and assign a bottle thermometer to each group. Do not allow them to touch their thermometer yet. Inform the participants that after you say "Ready, set, go!," each group must try to make the water shoot from the bottle as quickly as they can. The group that accomplishes this first is the winner. They can warm the bottles in whichever method they choose. For example, they can select warm-handed team members to hold the thermometer; they can rub the bottle; or they can breathe on the bottle.

A Homemade Barometer

A barometer is an important instrument used to predict weather. You can make a homemade barometer using simple household materials. You can test the barometer to see if it works, explain how it works, and even predict weather with it.

For this activity, you need:

- ○ an adult helper
- ○ a pop bottle with a plastic cap
- ○ scissors
- ○ a clear drinking straw or tubing
- ○ a rubber band
- ○ a homemade handle
- ○ water

To do this activity:

Ask an adult to help you make a hole in the plastic cap of the bottle large enough for the straw. Twist the tip of one scissor blade to make the hole. Insert the straw through the hole. Adjust the straw so one end almost touches the bottom of the bottle. Seal the straw with rubber cement so no air can leak through. Tie a rubber band near the bottom of the straw.

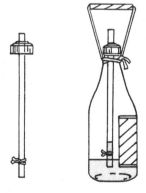

Fill the bottle with water so the water level in the straw is level with the rubber band when the cap is on. Cap the pop bottle tightly. Now make a handle as shown in the illustration.

From *Showy Science* published by GoodYearBooks. Copyright ©1994 by Hy Kim.

How do you know if the barometer is working? Carry it by its handle to a building with at least three floors. (If you carry the bottle in your hand, the air will be warmed by your body. Then the barometer will not record accurately because the temperature will have changed.)

Go to the bottom floor and check the water level. Then take the barometer up to the higher floors of the building. Check the water level on each floor. You can even use an elevator instead of walking up the stairs. Whichever way you choose, check the water level on the lowest floor and on the highest floor. You will be surprised at how much the water level changes in the column. The water level will rise on higher floors and go down on lower floors.

A barometer measures air pressure. At home, record your barometric readings for a few weeks. Compare them to the readings published in the local newspaper. You will discover that a decrease in air pressure will bring rain. An increase in air pressure will bring pleasant weather.

Why does this happen?

Air has weight just like water. If you dive into deep water, you feel pressure on your eardrums. In the same manner, you will feel pressure on your eardrums when you move up or down in an elevator, when you drive a car on a high mountain road, or when you ride on an airplane that is taking off or landing. We live at the bottom of an air ocean. There are about 15 pounds of pressure in every direction on every square inch! We do not feel it because we have an equal pressure that is inside us pushing out.

When you take your barometer to the basement, the air pressure outside of the bottle is greater than inside the bottle. The greater pressure pushes down the water level, equalizing the pressure. The air pressure is lower on the higher floors of your home. The air pressure inside the bottle is higher, pushing up the level of the water column.

By using a barometer to measure the air pressure in different regions, weather forecasters keep track of different air masses and their movements and they predict accordingly. A decrease in air pressure usually means bad weather is coming. An increase in air pressure usually means fair weather can be expected.

The Simplest Homemade Barometer

For this activity, you need:

○ water

○ a wide-mouthed jar

○ a bottle that will fit in the mouth of the jar (size does not matter, but the bottle must have a slender, long neck in order to show the water level changing)

To do this activity:

Fill the jar so that the water level covers the opening of the bottle's neck. (You can add food coloring to the water to make it more visible.)

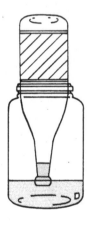

Invert the long-necked bottle and place it in the jar of water. The water level will be very low.

How does this barometer work?

By observing the water's movement in the bottle, you can measure the change in air pressure. If the air pressure increases, the water level in the bottle's neck will go up. This is the opposite direction from the pop bottle barometer's movement. If air pressure decreases, the water level in the bottle will go down. The air pressure inside the bottle will push the water level down, equalizing the air pressure between the inside and the outside of the bottle.

From *Showy Science* published by GoodYearBooks. Copyright ©1994 by Hy Kim.

How to Make an Altimeter

An altimeter measures altitude. An airplane pilot can tell how high his or her plane is flying just by reading an altimeter. In this activity, you will make your own altimeter based on the barometers you have built. Your homemade barometers can work as altimeters, too—you know this because you noticed a change in your barometer when you moved from your basement to a higher floor in an earlier activity.

For this activity, you need:

- ○ an adult helper
- ○ scissors
- ○ an apple cider jug with a cap
- ○ about 60 centimeters of clear plastic tubing
- ○ water
- ○ a lined index card
- ○ transparent tape
- ○ string or fabric
- ○ glue

To do this activity:

Ask an adult to help you make a hole in the middle of the cap. Insert one end of the tubing through this hole. Glue the tubing to seal it in the hole in the cap. Tape or glue an index card to the side of the bottle. Put the cap on the bottle and tighten it. Put one or two water drops in the tubing. Tape the tubing to the bottle as shown in the illustration. Make a handle with any string or fabric. The handle allows you to carry the altimeter without touching the bottle.

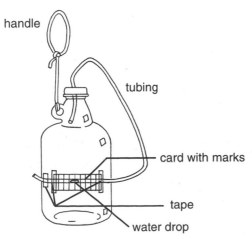

handle

tubing

card with marks

tape

water drop

To see if your altimeter works, run up and down a few flights of stairs. Watch the movement of the water drop.

How does this altimeter work?

It works the same way the other barometers work; only this device is intended to measure differences in air pressure caused by changes in altitude. It works well as a barometer, too!

A Tornado Machine

Two empty plastic pop bottles and some water provide the ideal conditions for a tornado machine. These conditions will produce the funnel shape of a tornado twister that will touch down inside your machine.

For this activity, you need:

○ an adult helper

○ a two-liter pop bottle with a plastic cap

○ a three-liter pop bottle

○ rubber cement

○ a few rubber bands

○ scissors

To do this activity:

Ask an adult to help you make a dime-sized hole on the plastic cap of the two-liter bottle. This can be done by twisting one blade of the scissors into the middle of the cap.

Tighten the cap onto the two-liter bottle. Put rubber cement around the outside, but not the top, of the cap. Take the three-liter bottle and put some rubber cement inside its mouth. Insert the two-liter bottle cap (the one you covered with rubber cement) into the mouth of the three-liter bottle. Wait until the rubber cement dries, sealing the cap inside the mouth of the three-liter bottle. Twist off the two-liter bottle. Wrap one or two rubber bands around the neck of the two-liter bottle like a rubber washer.

From *Showy Science* published by GoodYearBooks. Copyright ©1994 by Hy Kim.

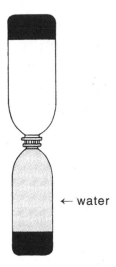

← water

To make it work, fill the two-liter bottle with water. Place the empty three-liter bottle on top of the other bottle. Twist tightly. Nothing will happen yet. Now, invert the bottles so that the water-filled two-liter bottle is on top of the empty three-liter bottle. Water from the top bottle will fall into the bottom bottle. (To make a tornado machine with two two-liter bottles, use tubing that fits the mouth of the bottles to connect them.)

Rotate the water-filled bottle in a counterclockwise, circular motion. The water will begin whirling, forming a funnel-shaped column of air in the center.

Why does this happen?

The water in the top bottle is heavier than the air in the bottom bottle. The water started falling while the air began moving upward. When you moved the bottle in a circular motion, the water descended in a circular motion, too. This left an air passage in the middle through which the air quickly ascended.

The water represents a dry, heavy, cold air mass. The air in the bottle represents a warm, moist air mass. When a warm air mass meets a cold air mass, the cold air usually moves underneath the warm air. However, under certain conditions, which scientists cannot explain, a cold air mass is sometimes pushed over a warm air mass. The lighter warm air mass, aided by strong winds, moves up through the cold air mass. This low pressure center in the cold air mass becomes a vortex which forms a funnel-shaped tornado.

Why does a tornado turn counterclockwise? The earth rotates on its axis, creating day and night. If you turn a globe while looking down at the Northern Hemisphere, the globe turns counterclockwise.

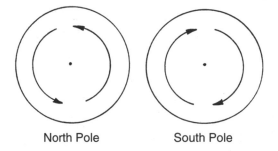

North Pole   South Pole

The earth's rotation contributes to the swirling movement of the tornado. However, if you look at the Southern Hemisphere while the globe is turning, the earth rotates clockwise. Therefore, tornadoes in the Southern Hemisphere turn clockwise.

From *Showy Science* published by GoodYearBooks. Copyright ©1994 by Hy Kim.

The Breathing Lung Model

Did you ever see a lung model that demonstrates breathing? It is very cheap and easy to make, and it clearly demonstrates the breathing mechanisms of your lungs. Your diaphragm is pushed down as your lungs inhale. As your lungs exhale, your diaphragm is pushed up.

For this activity, you need:

○ an adult helper

○ a two-liter plastic pop bottle

○ two balloons (representing lungs)

○ two flexible drinking straws (representing bronchial tubes)

○ a plastic sandwich bag (representing the diaphragm)

○ thread or rubber bands

○ scissors

To do this activity:

To make the model, first peel off the label and clean off the glue. (Soak it overnight in water to which a small amount of liquid detergent has been added.) Now, cut the plastic bottle along the black bottom.

← cut here

The bottom part will be shaped like a small cup. Have an adult help you drill a few holes on the bottom of the bottle. The holes on the black portion allow air to pass from the inside of the cup to the outside. Cover the black cup-shaped portion with a plastic bag as in the next illustration. Secure the bag by taping it to the black part. This represents the diaphragm of the lung model.

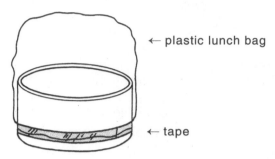

← plastic lunch bag

← tape

Now make a lung. Use thread or a rubber band to secure a balloon onto the bent end of a drinking straw. Make another lung by repeating the same steps.

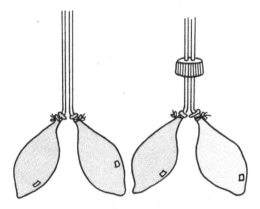

Make two holes in the plastic cap of the bottle. Insert the long, straight ends of the straws as in the illustration. The bent ends of the straws represent the bronchial tubes. The tied-together straws represent the trachea, which is the windpipe leading from the throat to the bronchial tubes.

Place the lungs inside the bottle, and tighten the cap. Now place the diaphragm on the open bottom of the bottle. Push the black cup-shaped portion onto the bottle as shown in the illustration below and seal it with tape. Your lung model is now completed.

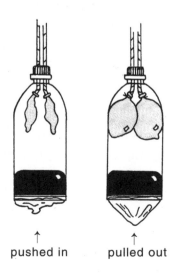

pushed in   pulled out

How does the model work?

Pull down and push up on the diaphragm of the model. Air will inflate and deflate the lungs. When you pull down the diaphragm, low air pressure in the chest cavity (bottle) will cause air pressure from the outside to push air into the lungs. When you push up on the diaphragm, high air pressure in the chest cavity will push the air out of the lungs.

The rib cage in your chest also helps you inhale and exhale as it expands and contracts. Your respiratory system does not have a large air pocket between the lungs and the diaphragm as shown in the model, but the principle is the same.

When you inhale, oxygen-rich air fills millions of tiny air sacs in your lungs. Tiny blood vessels called *capillaries* surround each of these air sacs. Oxygen molecules combine with red blood cells through the capillary walls. Carbon dioxide gas leaves the blood cells by passing out into the air to be exhaled. The oxygen-rich blood goes to your heart and then circulates around your body, providing oxygen to your cells.

The cells get energy by combining the oxygen with food. They give off water, carbon dioxide and other wastes to the blood. The blood carries away the wastes, getting rid of the carbon dioxide in the lungs. The blood deposits water and other waste in the kidneys.

If you run, you use more oxygen and food than if you walk or sit down. Therefore, you have to breathe more frequently to supply more oxygen and to get rid of carbon dioxide. You can demonstrate this rapid breathing you do when you exercise by pulling and pushing the diaphragm rapidly.

Breathing Plants

Place a jar containing a water plant and some water in a sunny place. Soon you will see bubbles rising from the plant. The stream of bubbles stop rising if you remove the jar from sunlight. This demonstration shows that plants breathe, allowing you to explore the concept of photosynthesis in green plants.

For this activity, you need:

○ a transparent jar (an apple cider jar is highly recommended)

○ some water plants (such as hornwort, which is available at a pet shop)

○ a paper clip

○ plenty of sunshine or a bright lamp

○ a pinch of baking soda

To do this activity:

Fill the jar with water. Place the water plants inside. (You will obtain the best results if your plant is young and healthy.) Add a pinch of baking soda to the water. If the jar is tall, put a paper clip on the bottom of the plant's stem so the plant floats upright in the water.

shooting air bubbles

Expose the jar to direct light. Bright sunlight is recommended. On a cloudy day, use a bright lamp instead. In the classroom, you can use an overhead projector as the light source.

Watch the plant. At first, you will see many small bubbles surface from the spot where you cut the plant. Later, they will emerge from all over the plant.

Now place the jar in the shade and keep watching for the bubbles. The plant will stop producing bubbles. If you place the jar back in direct sunlight, the plant will produce bubbles again.

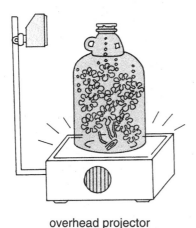

overhead projector

Why does this happen?

Someone may exclaim, "I didn't know that plants breathe like animals!" What really happens to the plants is a chemical change called *photosynthesis*. In photosynthesis, green plants combine carbon dioxide gas and water, forming sugar molecules. When green plants undergo photosynthesis, they release oxygen bubbles as a by-product of the process. Sugar molecules stay in the plant, and oxygen molecules leave as a gas. When plants release oxygen gas, the gas rises to the water surface because gas is lighter than water.

A pinch of baking soda in the water provides carbon dioxide for the plants. A small amount of carbon dioxide is almost always present in air and water. However, by providing additional carbon dioxide to the experiment, the oxygen formation is more easily accomplished.

About 20 percent of ordinary air is oxygen. Photosynthesis by green plants helps maintain this constant ratio.

All animals need oxygen to live. When we inhale, we take in oxygen from the air and release carbon dioxide into the air. On the other hand, green plants use carbon dioxide from the air in their food-making process and release oxygen into the air. Green plants and animals are good partners on earth.

From *Showy Science* published by GoodYearBooks. Copyright ©1994 by Hy Kim.

A Collection of Oxygen Bubbles

You can collect the oxygen bubbles in a bottle and do some fantastic experiments.

For this activity, you need:

- ○ an adult helper
- ○ a large bottle (or jar) with water plants and a screw-on cap
- ○ water
- ○ a hammer
- ○ a nail
- ○ a pinch of baking soda
- ○ a small bottle (or jar)
- ○ a piece of paper
- ○ a pie pan or towel

To do this activity:

Make a hole in the center of the large bottle's cap. Have an adult help you use a hammer to pound a large nail through the inside of the cap to the outside so that the torn, sharp edges face outward. Be careful!

Add a pinch of baking soda to the water. Now screw the cap onto the large bottle containing water and water plants.

Pour in more water through the nail hole until the bottle is completely filled. Now set the bottle in a pie pan or on a towel to catch any spilled water.

Fill the small bottle to the top with water. Cover its opening with a piece of paper. Flip the bottle over and place it on top of the large bottle's cap. Slowly pull the paper out from between the jars.

From *Showy Science* published by GoodYearBooks. Copyright ©1994 by Hy Kim.

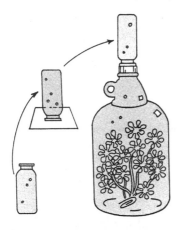

Now the oxygen-collecting device is completed. Place the device in a spot where the green plants can receive direct light. Tiny bubbles will rise to the top of the small bottle through the nail hole. As the air bubbles accumulate in the top of the bottle, some water will seep out between the two bottles.

A Spectacular Fire Flame

If you set up the oxygen-collecting device on a sunny spring or summer day, you may be able to collect a small bottle of oxygen in just one day. Or you can leave the device under a light overnight to collect gas in the bottle. You can prove that the gas is oxygen with the following spectacular demonstration.

For this activity, you need:

○ an adult helper
○ the oxygen-collecting device from the last activity

To do this activity:

Wait until the oxygen-collecting bottle is full. Then insert a piece of paper between the two bottles. Flip over the bottle while holding the paper in place. Now you are ready to show the fire flame.

Ask an adult to light a wooden splinter or match and blow out the flame, as in the illustration. Now insert the glowing part of the match into the bottle.

The glowing part will suddenly ignite with a weak "pop" sound. Hold the oxygen bottle open-side-up to prevent the gas from escaping.

Why does this happen?

This activity not only proves that the gas is oxygen, but it also provides a fascinating eye catcher! Oxygen gas is heavier than ordinary air, which is about 78 percent nitrogen and 21 percent oxygen.

Rusting Steel Wool

How can you prove that about 20 percent of ordinary air is oxygen? This simple experiment will prove it.

For this activity, you need:

○ a small amount of steel wool

○ a ruler

○ a small jar of vinegar

○ water

○ a wide-mouthed jar

○ a pencil

○ a test tube (if you do not have a test tube, a medicine vial or
  small bottle will work, too)

To do this activity:

Measure the length of the test tube with a ruler. Divide the measurement by 5. Take that number and find its distance from the opening of the tube. Mark this 1/5-point length with a marker or a rubber band as in the next illustration. This marker will indicate the 20 percent point of the tube's content.

Make a steel wool ball that is slightly larger in diameter than the test tube, so it will not fall to the bottom of the tube when you place it inside. Form the ball loosely. Do

From *Showy Science* published by GoodYearBooks. Copyright ©1994 by Hy Kim.

not squeeze the steel wool too tightly; make sure that air can reach all parts of the steel wool. Place the ball in a jar filled with vinegar. Submerge the ball in the vinegar for about 5 minutes.

Now fill the wide-mouthed jar with about 3 centimeters of water. Remove the steel wool ball from the vinegar. Shake it out in the air so that the steel wool contains no drops of vinegar. Insert the ball into the test tube. Push it to the middle of the test tube with a pencil. Quickly place the test tube upside-down in the wide-mouthed jar of water.

Watch the water level in the test tube. Over time, to everyone's surprise, the water level will continue to go up until it reaches your mark. Check the water level after one hour. The water level will have already reached the 20 percent mark. No matter how long you leave it set up, the level will not move beyond the mark.

How does this prove that 20 percent of ordinary air is oxygen?

When you placed the tube in the jar, the air inside the tube was trapped. The steel wool in the tube began a process of chemical change called "rusting" (*oxidation*). Some of its iron atoms combined with oxygen atoms to form rust. Rust forms only where there is oxygen.

When the oxygen atoms are in a gaseous state, they take up a lot of space. When the oxygen atoms in this demonstration became part of a solid (rust), their volume decreased so drastically that we could not recognize them.

As a result of oxygen's change from gas to solid, a vacuum was formed in the tube. This change reduced the air pressure inside the tube. The higher outside atmospheric pressure pushed water into the tube, equalizing the air pressure inside and outside. Exposing the steel wool to vinegar accelerated the rusting process.

Does a Solid Expand When Heated?

Not only gas and water expand when they are heated and contract when they are cooled. Solids do, too. You can demonstrate that a solid also expands when hot and contracts when cold.

For this activity, you need:

- ○ a meter stick
- ○ a meter length of copper wire (#16 size is recommended)
- ○ a wire coat hanger
- ○ tape
- ○ a plain piece of paper
- ○ a hair dryer
- ○ two nails or large thumbtacks

To do this activity:

Suspend the copper wire along the meter stick by hooking the top end over a nail. Make another hook at the other end of the wire. Ask an adult to help you cut a coat hanger. Straighten its wire and make a bend and a loop in the end as shown in the illustration. Place the bend in the wire hanger on the hook of the vertical copper wire as in the illustration. Have an adult drive a nail through the loop in the coat hanger wire and into the meter stick.

From *Showy Science* published by GoodYearBooks. Copyright ©1994 by Hy Kim.

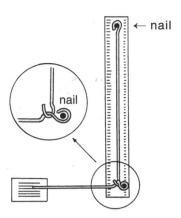

Now tape the meter stick to a wall. Place a plain piece of paper behind the coat hanger wire. Make a mark where the wire rests on this paper. Using a hair dryer, heat the copper wire. Watch the coat hanger wire indicator move as the copper wire grows hotter. The indicator will move down from your earlier mark. Mark the paper at this new point as well. Shut off the hair dryer and watch how the indicator moves up. Your friends will be impressed and convinced that solids expand and contract according to temperature.

You can make a portable version of this device, but it is smaller in scale and in a wooden frame. You can move this device from a hot place to a cool one and notice the indicator's change.

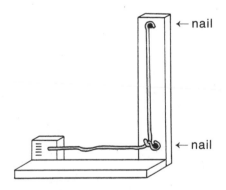

This can work as a thermometer if you mark the varying degrees of temperature.

Why does this work?

The copper wire expands as it is heated and contracts as it cools. The slow change and the small range of movement make it hard for us to detect a change. The coat hanger wire magnifies the movement with its long arm. This device makes the process much easier to see.

A Great Bet!

Because invisible air pressure always surrounds us, some activities using air pressure appear mysterious. In this activity, no one in your audience will be able to blow a small balloon out of a funnel. Blowing hard into the funnel will only make the ball stick more to the bottom. In order to perform the balloon-ball stunts, you must construct a simple system like the one described in this activity.

For this activity, you need:

- ○ a two-liter pop bottle
- ○ a drill (ask an adult to help you use it)
- ○ a flexible drinking straw
- ○ a piece of tissue paper
- ○ a small balloon or Ping Pong ball
- ○ a pair of scissors

To do this activity:

Use your scissors to cut off the upper portion of the plastic pop bottle. This upper part makes a funnel as shown on the next page. Ask an adult to drill a hole big enough to insert the drinking straw in the middle of the plastic cap. Tightly screw the cap onto the funnel.

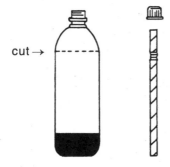

cut →

Insert the short end of the flexible straw through the hole. Inflate a small balloon to the size of a tennis ball and tie it. (You can use a Ping Pong ball in place of a balloon.) Place the balloon in the open part of the funnel. Adjust the straw so that its end does not touch the balloon. Your system is now ready.

From *Showy Science* published by GoodYearBooks. Copyright ©1994 by Hy Kim.

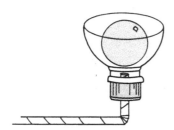

Hold the system so that the funnel faces upward. Announce to your audience that anybody who can blow the balloon out of the funnel will win a fabulous prize. (You can offer any prize and you will never lose the bet! It is that certain!) Ask volunteers to blow the balloon out of the funnel. Do not allow them to change the funnel's position. To everybody's surprise, the balloon will not come out of the funnel!

Why does this happen?

We live in an ocean of air that exerts tremendous air pressure upon us in all directions. Fast-moving air or water which speeds up by itself will exert less pressure. Therefore, air that moves quickly from the end of the straw has less pressure than the stationary surrounding air. The greater air pressure that surrounds the fast-moving airstream pushes on the balloon. If an air mass moves faster and faster, it will exert less and less air pressure. As a result, the air pressure from the still or slow-moving air mass pushes into the rapidly moving air mass. This phenomena is called *Bernoulli's principle*.

A Balloon-Ball Stunt

In this demonstration, no one in your audience will be able to blow the balloon out of the funnel, even though the funnel faces downward.

For this activity, you need:

○ the system you created in the last activity

To do this activity:

Hold the system that you created earlier so that the funnel faces downward. Support the balloon in the funnel with your hand. Blow a steady stream of air through the straw. Release your hand from the balloon. What happens?

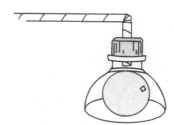

You may think that the balloon will fall out because of gravity, but it sticks to the funnel!

To do a similar activity:

Let's look at another demonstration in which you will use a hair dryer to produce a stream of rapidly moving air. To begin, remove the cap and the straw from the funnel. Place the balloon on the table and cover it with the funnel. Turn on the hair dryer and blow a stream of air down through the throat of the funnel.

Lift up the funnel and the hair dryer. The balloon will be stuck to the funnel instead of blown out. Turn off the dryer, and the balloon will drop out of the funnel.

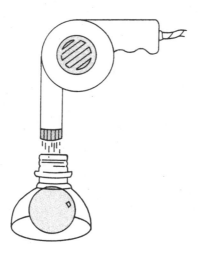

What happens in these activities?

As in the previous activity, Bernoulli's principle explains why the balloon stays in the funnel in these activities.

From *Showy Science* published by GoodYearBooks. Copyright ©1994 by Hy Kim.

Blow the Balloon Out of the Funnel Easily!

You, the magician, can show your audience that you can easily blow the balloon out of the funnel. You can also make the balloon hover in the air.

For this activity, you need:

○ the system you used in the last activity

To do this activity:

Trick your audience by changing the length of the straw that is in the funnel. Show them that the balloon will either float in the air or remain at the bottom of the funnel at your command.

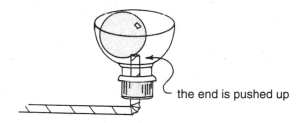

the end is pushed up

Expose a little more of the straw in the funnel. Blow forcefully through the straw. You can easily blow the balloon out of the funnel. Pull the straw back so that it does not touch the balloon. Blow into the straw once again. This time, the balloon will stick to the funnel.

From *Showy Science* published by GoodYearBooks. Copyright ©1994 by Hy Kim.

The Hovering Balloon

You can make the balloon fly mysteriously above the funnel without falling. It looks like invisible hands are holding the balloon in the air as you blow through the straw.

For this activity, you need:

○ the same materials you used in the previous activities

To do this activity:

Hold the balloon about 10 to 20 centimeters above the funnel. Take a deep breath. Blow a steady stream of air into the funnel. As you do this, release the balloon. As the steady stream of air pushes on the balloon, it will float above the funnel. It will remain there as long as you keep blowing in air.

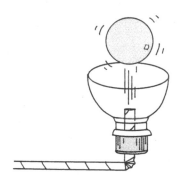

For a similar activity, you need:

○ a desk or screen
○ a balloon
○ a hair dryer

To do this activity:

You can make a balloon float in the middle of the room without falling or flying away. The hovering balloon will move back and forth, left and right, all by your command!

Perform this activity behind a desk or a screen. Inflate a balloon and tie the opening closed. Turn on your hair dryer without showing the audience, and hold it with one hand so that the stream of air flows straight up. (Remember, don't show the dryer to

From *Showy Science* published by GoodYearBooks. Copyright ©1994 by Hy Kim.

your audience!) Place the balloon in the middle of the airstream above the desk. Release it right above the airstream. The balloon will rise or fall depending upon the speed of the airstream, but it will remain in the airstream as long as the dryer is turned on and pointed up.

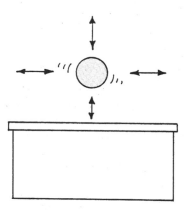

Command your balloon by saying, "My magic balloon, move to the right side!" Move the hair dryer slowly to the right side. The balloon will follow by moving to the right side. You can move the balloon to the left, forward, and backward using the same method. The balloon will also go up if you turn the dryer on high power. The balloon will go down if you switch the dryer to low power.

Why do these activities work this way?

The moving airstream pushes the balloon to a height where the force of the air equals the weight of the balloon. When the dryer is switched to low power, the force is less because of the reduced speed. The balloon then falls until the forces are equal again. That is why the balloon can hover in the air without falling.

The Atomizer

A simple atomizer can spray a fine shower of water on your friend's hands. It can also spray water colors to use in coloring a picture.

For this activity, you need:

- ○ a bottle filled with water
- ○ two drinking straws

To do this activity:

Cut a drinking straw into two unequal lengths. Insert the shorter one into the bottle of water.

Hold each straw as in the illustration. Hold the longer straw at a right angle. Blow through it and see what happens. Adjust the distance and positions of the straws so that you can spray the water efficiently. You can spray many tiny water droplets through this atomizer system. If the audience cannot see the water spray, ask one volunteer to place his or her hand in front of the atomizer in order to feel the spray.

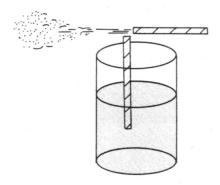

Create beautiful and unusual pictures by spraying watercolors. Mix ink or watercolor paint in the bottle. Blow into the straw to spray colors on to a piece of paper.

Why does this work?

As you blow air through the longer straw, a mass of air moves very quickly over the other straw. This creates low air pressure in the straw placed in the water. The air pressure that pushes down on the water surface is greater than the air pressure inside the small straw. This pressure pushes water into the small straw. When the water gets to the top, it is blown off in tiny water droplet sprays. A spray gun, airbrush, sandblaster, and paint gun work on this same principle.

From *Showy Science* published by GoodYearBooks. Copyright ©1994 by Hy Kim.

Spinning Soda Cans

For this activity, you need:

○ a straw
○ two empty soda cans
○ string
○ a ruler

To do this activity:

Tie a string to the tab of each empty soda can. Suspend the cans on a ruler as shown below. The length of the string between the can and the ruler should be about 15 centimeters. The distance between the two cans should be about 3 centimeters. Place the ruler on the edge of a table. Put some weights over the end of the ruler to stabilize the system.

Ask your audience what will happen when you blow a stream of air directly between the two cans. Some might predict that the cans will fly apart as the airstream forces them apart.

Hold one end of the straw about 3 centimeters in front of the cans. Aim the straw halfway between them. Blow a steady airstream through the straw. Watch what happens.

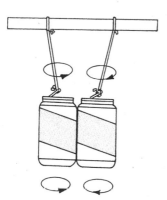

The two cans will slowly move toward each other and spin.

Why does this happen?

The spinning can be explained with Bernoulli's principle: The airstream exerts a force on the sides of the cans that are close together. The weight of the cans and air pressure keeps them from blowing outward or back. The result is that the two cans spin, one clockwise and the other counterclockwise.

A Pop Bottle Whistle

In this activity, you can make a whistling sound by blowing across the top of a pop bottle. You can even make a whistling sound by cupping your hands.

For this activity, you need:

○ several different sizes of pop bottles
○ a drinking straw

To do this activity:

Blow across the top of a pop bottle to make a sound.

Try to make the same sound by blowing through a drinking straw.

Why does this happen?

In this activity, an important role is played by "overshoot." Overshoot occurs when something goes beyond what is expected or needed. Air is rushing out of the bottle as you blow across it. The pressure inside the bottle drops. Soon, the pressure outside of the bottle is higher than the pressure inside of the bottle. The amount of air that left the bottle was more than was needed to make the pressure inside and outside the bottle the same. Air rushes in to fill the bottle. This caused the pressure inside the bottle to rise and go beyond, or overshoot, the pressure outside the bottle. Through this movement of air, the air column in the bottle vibrates back and forth, making a sound.

From *Showy Science* published by GoodYearBooks. Copyright ©1994 by Hy Kim.

A Pop Bottle Musical Instrument

For this activity, you need:

○ water

○ a drinking straw

○ several identical pop bottles

To do this activity:

Add different amounts of water to the bottles. To tune your bottles to the musical scale, use a straw to add or remove water as needed. Try to create some simple tunes.

Why does this work?

The increasing amounts of water make a smaller air column in each bottle. When an air column is small, it vibrates more frequently as you blow. This produces a higher pitched sound.

A Cupped-Hands Whistle

You can make a whistling sound with your own hands!

For this activity, you need:

○ your hands

To do this activity:

Cup your hands as shown in the illustration. Notice that the cup has a small opening, shown by the dark shape between your thumbs. Place your lips on the spot indicated by the arrow.

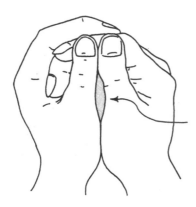

Blow through the opening while adjusting the angle of the cupped-hands to your lips. Eventually you will get the right angle and make a loud whistling sound.

Why does this happen?

This cupped-hands whistle works on the same principle as the pop bottle whistle.

Whistling Sounds by a Whirling Bottle

¡S!

You can make a whistling sound by whirling a bottle that is tied to a string in the air.

For this activity, you need:

○ a plastic bottle about the size of a small orange juice bottle (this should have a larger mouth than a pop bottle)
○ a durable string

To do this activity:

Tie a string on the neck of the plastic bottle as in the illustration. Make sure the knot is secure. You don't want it to come loose while you whirl the bottle through the air.

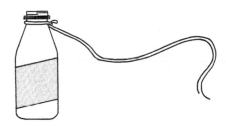

Now hold the string tightly, and whirl the bottle around. Vary the speed of the whirling. Listen for a humming sound. You may be able to produce a sound that some whales make in the ocean! (Glass bottles will also make the same humming sound, but they are not safe to use. Never whirl a glass bottle!)

Why does it work? The same principle that makes a sound when you blow across the mouth of the bottle applies in this activity. This time you do not actually blow the airstream across the mouth of the bottle, but you whirl the bottle rapidly. As a result of this whirling, air moves quickly across the mouth of the bottle.

A Model Ear

Sounds are made because something vibrates or moves rapidly. Can you show the vibration of sound? There are many ways to visualize vibrations such as flicking a stretched rubber band which makes a sound, or by placing some sand grains on a drum which will vibrate when beaten. You can make an ear model to demonstrate how sound changes into water waves. This will show you how your ears work.

For this activity, you need:

- ○ a cardboard tube (about 10 centimeters in diameter)
- ○ a paper dish for the outer ear
- ○ glue
- ○ a piece of thin paper for the ear drum
- ○ a paper clip
- ○ about 12 centimeters of thin wire
- ○ a rubber band
- ○ a transparent water container
- ○ an overhead projector

To do this activity:

Glue a piece of paper to one end of the cardboard tube by putting glue around the rim of the tube and standing it on a piece of paper. After the glue is dry, trim the excess paper around the tube. (This paper simulates an ear drum.)

Next, glue the other end of the tube to the center of the paper plate. Now use a sharp knife to cut a hole through the plate, exposing the inside of the tube. (The plate represents the outer ear, or the part of the ear that you can see.)

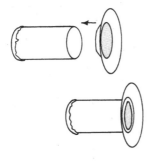

Now hold the model ear over a radio speaker, as in the illustration, and place some grains of rice or sand on the ear drum. Next, turn on the radio loudly and observe the sand grains vibrate on the ear drum.

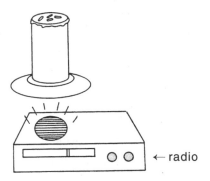

← radio

To make this sound, first the speaker vibrated. Next, the air molecules vibrated because they were activated by the vibrating speaker. In turn, the ear drum vibrated. Finally, the sand grains vibrated in response to the vibrating ear drum. To make a representation of the inner ear, wrap a piece of wire three times around one end of a paper clip (shown in the circle). Attach the paper clip to the ear canal (the cardboard tube part of the ear) by inserting the paper clip under a rubber band that has been placed around the canal, making sure that the straight part of the wire (representing the stirrup bone in the middle ear) extends outward from the canal.

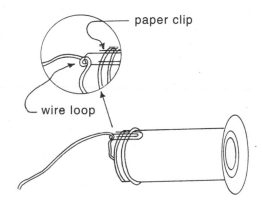

paper clip

wire loop

Place a transparent container with about 2 millimeters of water in it on the stage of an overhead projector. Position the ear model on the stage of the overhead so that the stirrup barely touches the surface of the center of the water. Place some sup- porters on both sides of the ear model so that the model is stable. Turn on the projector, darken the room, and provide a loud sound aimed at the outer ear.

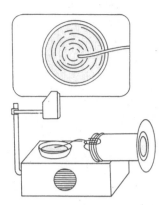

Turning on a radio or striking a tuning fork is a good way to provide a loud sound. The vibration of sound will transfer to the stirrup and it will cause a wave motion in the water that can be seen by all in the room.

How does the ear work?

The parts of an actual ear and the model ear are shown below.

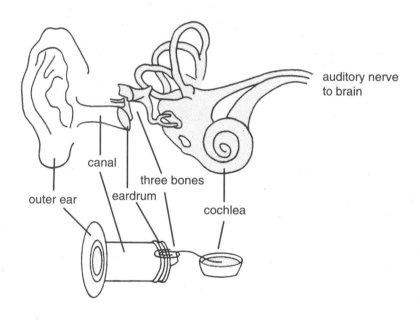

Vibrations in the air are guided to the ear canal by the outer ear. Then the sound waves vibrate the ear drum. These vibrations are transferred to the three bones (the hammer, the anvil, and the stirrup), and finally to the cochlea. The coiled cochlea of the inner ear contains liquid. When the cochlea vibrates, the liquid moves. Receptors detect the motion of the liquid and transmit electrical signals to the auditory nerve. Signals move along this nerve to the hearing center of the brain where the signals are interpreted as sounds.

A Hot-Air Balloon

Making and launching a hot-air balloon is an exciting way to demonstrate convection currents in air. However, doing this tissue-paper project involves a lot of work! Therefore, it is a good project for your whole family or class.

For this activity, you need:

- O fifteen sheets of tissue paper for one balloon (You can buy different colors of tissue paper in gift and card stores. A selection of contrasting bright colors will make the balloon more attractive. Several different sizes of tissue paper are available also. For our purposes, the 51 centimeters by 66 centimeters (approximately 20 x 26 inches) size is best.)
- O a bottle of white glue
- O scissors
- O a small camping stove
- O a meter of stovepipe with a 10-centimeter diameter (4 inches)
- O a piece of construction paper

To do this activity:

Glue the fifteen pieces of colored tissue paper together to make five larger pieces. These will form the sides of the balloon. Begin by gluing three pieces of tissue paper along their 51 centimeter sides (with a 0.5 centimeter overlap). These will form a large rectangular panel about 197 centimeters long and 51 centimeters wide.

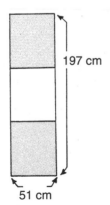

197 cm

51 cm

Make four additional panels in the same manner, allowing the glue to dry before attempting to move them.

Fold each panel vertically as shown in the next illustration. Draw a smooth arc from the edge of the second tissue to the center fold of the top. Draw another arc in the same way from the bottom to the middle as shown.

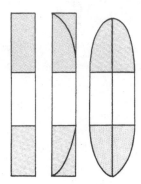

Cut along the arch, and unfold the panel. It should look like the picture above. Follow the same directions to make four more ballon parts.

To assemble the balloon, lay one panel on a large, clean surface. Lay a second panel on top of the first, leaving 3 to 5 millimeters of the bottom panel exposed on the left, as shown below.

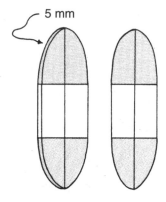

Apply a thin layer of glue to the exposed area on the bottom panel. Then fold the glued area up and over the top panel, and press down the freshly glued fold. Repeat these steps with panels 3, 4, and 5. Fold and glue the two remaining panel sides (panels 1 and 5) together in the same manner to complete the sides of the balloon.

From *Showy Science* published by GoodYearBooks. Copyright ©1994 by Hy Kim.

With a two-centimeter-wide strip of construction paper, make a ring through which the stovepipe can be inserted. Cut off the bottom tip of the tissue balloon. Glue the ring to the balloon to reinforce the opening. Attach a few tissue-paper strips to the ring.

To launch your balloon, you will need a camping stove with one burner and a stovepipe about 1 meter (3 feet) in height and 10 centimeters (4 inches) in diameter. A pipe holder over the stove is handy. Two coat hanger wires are used to construct this holder.

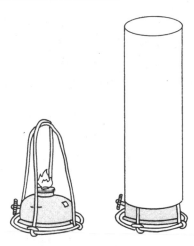

Cool mornings and evenings in the spring or fall are best for hot-air balloon launches. The summer is not a good season for launching tissue-paper balloons because it is very difficult to make the balloon air hotter than the outside air. Set up the launching station in an open space such as a park or a playground.

Have an adult help you ignite the stove. Now cage the stove with the pipe holder and slide the pipe down over the holder.

Deflate the balloon. Slide the balloon's ring over the pipe. As the balloon inflates with hot air, keep the balloon vertical by supporting the top of the balloon. This will enable hot air to move easily into the balloon.

As hot air fills the balloon, the balloon will rise. At this time, you should release it. The balloon will rise and move with the wind. It will eventually land once the hot air cools.

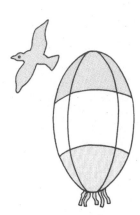

Occasionally, the balloon will turn upside-down and fall to the ground. This is probably caused by insufficient weight at the bottom. To remedy this, you can attach more tissue paper strips to the ring, thereby adding more weight. If the balloon develops a hole, patch it with more tissue paper.

How does the balloon work?

Hot air molecules move faster and take up more space than the same mass of cold air molecules. Therefore, a liter of warm air is lighter than a liter of cold air. When they meet, warm air rises over cold air. The weight of the hot air balloon is lighter than the same volume of surrounding air, causing it to rise.

From *Showy Science* published by GoodYearBooks. Copyright ©1994 by Hy Kim.

ACTIVITIES FOR
EXPLORING

WATER

The Water Trick

Everybody knows that water will spill out of a glass if you hold the glass upside-down. However, if you place an index card on the mouth of the glass and hold it upside-down, the water won't pour out! Try to find the minimum amount of water in the glass that you need for this activity.

For this activity, you need:

○ a glass
○ index cards
○ water

To do this activity:

Partially fill two glasses with water and place an index card over the mouth of each, as in the illustration. Press the index card lightly to the glass with the palm of your hand, and gently flip over the glass so that the index card is positioned on the bottom.

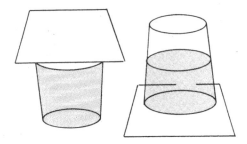

Slowly remove your hand from the card. The water will not spill! Try it again with a different amount of water.

Why does this work?

Because we live on the bottom of an "air ocean," there is a great amount of air pressure on everything on the earth's surface. A force equal to that exerted by a kilogram mass is on every square centimeter at sea level. This pressure also presses the glass from all directions. When gravity on the water pulls the water down, a partial vacuum is created inside the jar. This lowers the air pressure inside the glass. Outside air pressure presses upward against the index card, keeping the water from spilling. When this happens, it equalizes the forces inside and outside the jar.

Competition makes this activity even more fun. Give a glass and an index card to each of your friends. Ask them to do the same activity while trying to succeed with the least amount of water in the glass. The person who performs the activity with the least amount of water is the winner.

From *Showy Science* published by GoodYearBooks. Copyright ©1994 by Hy Kim.

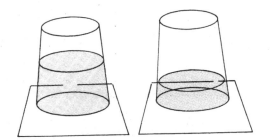

Why is it more difficult to keep a smaller amount of water in the glass? If you put only a little bit of water in the glass, the rest of the space inside is taken up by a larger amount of trapped air. Air can easily be compressed or expanded; a large amount of air can proportionally expand more than a small amount of air. The large pocket of trapped air in the glass exerts more pressure on the water. In turn, this pushes the index card away from the rim of the glass, allowing air to enter and the water to spill. This simple activity is related to the following useful device.

A Self-Refilling Water Bowl for Pets

If you have a pet, you know that you must keep putting fresh water in its bowl for it to drink. You can make a device that will refill the bowl with fresh water as the pet drinks. It will even keep the water level constant! By using this device, you free yourself from the chore of filling the bowl with fresh water every day.

For this activity, you need:

○ a large bottle (a gallon size is good)
○ a water dish
○ three small blocks that can be used to support the bottle

To do this activity:

Fill the bottle to the top with fresh water. Cover the bottle with the water dish so that the smooth bottom of the dish touches the mouth of the bottle. Carefully flip over the bottle and dish together, and place the device where your pet can find it. Lift up a corner of the bottle and insert the small blocks between the dish and the bottle. Water will flow into the water dish until the water level reaches exactly the height of the small blocks!

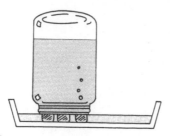

As your pet drinks, fresh water will flow into the dish, maintaining the same water level until all the water in the bottle is gone.

For a similar activity, you need:

○ an adult helper

○ an apple cider jug with cap

○ string

○ tape

○ water

○ a bowl

○ a drill

To do this activity:

With some durable string, make a harness by which you can suspend the jug as shown below.

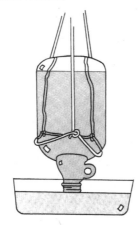

Fill the jug with water, and cap the jug temporarily. Using the harness you have made, suspend the jug from a convenient height. Place a water bowl directly underneath the jug's mouth. Make sure the mouth of the jug is below the rim of the dish. Now remove the jug's cap. Water will fill the bowl until it reaches the mouth of the jug. Whenever the water level goes down, fresh water will fill the bowl to the same water level.

You can use a two-liter pop bottle to make the water refilling device, too. As shown in the following illustration, make two holes in the bottle about 5 millimeters in size, one at the bottom and one at the side. Ask an adult to help you use an electric drill to make the holes.

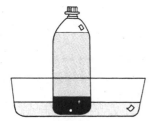

Block the holes with tape, and fill the bottle to the top with fresh water. Tighten the cap on the bottle and place it in a water dish as shown above. Remove the tape from the holes. You will see air bubbles rising in the bottle from the side hole. Water will flow through the bottom hole into the dish. When the water level reaches the side hole, both the water flow and the air bubbles will stop.

Why does this work?

If the water level goes down, a gap will form between the water level and the rim of the bottle. Through this gap, air seeps into the bottle and releases an equal volume of water into the dish. Once the water level reaches the rim of the bottle, the air passage is blocked, and the water stops flowing.

Water Jets I

Use the following illustration to set up this simple system.

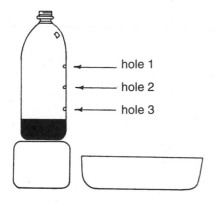

One hole will always shoot a longer stream, or jet, of water. Which hole is it? Ask your friends to predict the answer!

For this activity, you need:

- ○ an adult helper
- ○ a plastic pop bottle
- ○ water
- ○ a container
- ○ a block on which the bottle can stand

To do this activity:

Make three holes on the side of the bottle, one above the other. An adult can help you make these holes more easily by heating one end of a metal wire (such as a coat hanger) and applying the heated metal to the plastic bottle.

Plug the three holes with your fingers, and fill the bottle to the top with water. Place the bottle on a block. Place a container in front of the bottle to catch the water. As you prepare to demonstrate this to your friends, ask them, "Which hole will shoot a water jet the farthest?" Then release your fingers to see whose prediction is correct!

The results will be similar to the illustration. The bottom hole shoots the water jet the longest distance, the middle hole a little shorter, and the top hole the shortest distance of all.

Why is this? The bottom hole has more water above the hole, which creates more pressure on it than the other two holes. This is also why you feel more pressure when you dive to the bottom of a swimming pool compared to when you are just wading.

Cover the upper two holes with tape. Fill the bottle to the top. With the bottom hole exposed, watch how far the water jet shoots as the water level goes down.

From *Showy Science* published by GoodYearBooks. Copyright ©1994 by Hy Kim.

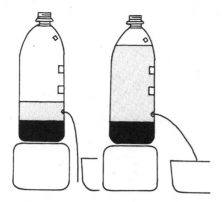

How does this happen?

The water jet becomes shorter as the water level goes down because the water pressure above the hole is diminishing.

Water Jets II

For this activity, you need:

○ the bottle from the last activity

To do this activity:

Take the bottle and plug its holes with your fingers. Fill it with water and tighten the cap. Before you release your fingers, predict what will happen with the water jets.

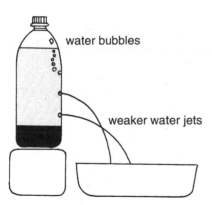

water bubbles

weaker water jets

Your results will be similar to the illustration above. The bottom two holes will produce weak water jets. The top hole will take in air, forming bubbles in the bottle. Why does the top hole make air bubbles in the water? Air pressure surrounding the bottle forces air inside through the top hole because it has the least water pressure.

Try to block the top hole with your finger. What happens? The middle hole makes air bubbles and the bottom hole makes a weak water jet.

For a similar activity, you need:

○ the bottle from the last activity

To do this activity:

As the water jets grow weaker, and only two streams are running, "pinch" the streams together. They will remain together. You may also tilt the bottle slightly so that the two water jet streams meet and become one.

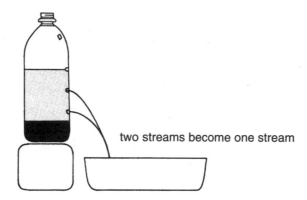

two streams become one stream

Why does this happen?

Like oppositely charged particles, water molecules attract each other. This attracting force between the water molecules is called *cohesive force*. This force keeps water in a liquid state instead of a gaseous one.

From *Showy Science* published by GoodYearBooks. Copyright ©1994 by Hy Kim.

A Series of Provoking Tasks

For this activity, you need:

○ the two-liter pop bottle from the previous experiment

To do this activity:

Fill the pop bottle to the top with water while blocking the holes with your fingers. Put the cap on the bottle and tighten it. Hold the bottle horizontally as shown below.

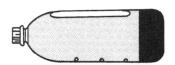

If you have an audience, ask them what they think will happen if you release your fingers from the holes. Release your fingers. What happens? Does one hole shoot a stronger water jet than the others?

Water doesn't flow out of any of the holes! Now, raise the right side of the bottle a little bit and see what happens. Do the same to the left side.

If you hold the bottle horizontally, no water will run out of the bottle.

Why does this happen?

This happens because the three holes have an equal force of water pressure on them. Water pressure tries to push the water out through the holes, but there is no weak hole through which air can go into the bottle. However, if you tilt one side of the bottle, the highest hole has the least water pressure on it. This allows the air to enter the bottle. The lower holes now permit the water to flow out of the bottle.

The Obedient Diver

You can make an eye-dropper diver system. The diver will obey your every command. If you order the diver to dive in the bottle, it will go down. If you order it to rise, it will.

For this activity, you need:

○ one two-liter pop bottle or any other kind of transparent plastic bottle
○ a glass eyedropper (your diver) (A plastic eyedropper won't work, but a test tube can be used instead of an eyedropper.)
○ an empty jar with a large mouth
○ water

To do this activity:

Fill an empty jar with water as shown below. Notice that if you place the eyedropper in the jar, it will float.

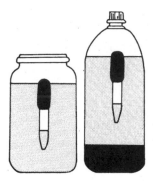

Squeeze and release the rubber bulb on the eyedropper to draw water into it. Do this until the rubber bulb touches the surface of the water when it is floated in the water.

Now fill the pop bottle about 3/4 full of water. Remove the eyedropper from the jar and drop it into the filled pop bottle. Tighten the cap on the bottle. You are now ready to demonstrate how the obedient diver works.

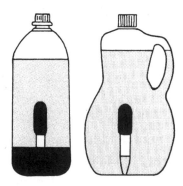

From *Showy Science* published by GoodYearBooks. Copyright ©1994 by Hy Kim.

Squeeze the bottle. What happens to the diver? The diver will sink. As you release the bottle, the diver will float. Pretend you have magical powers to make the diver float or sink. Do this while you squeeze and release the bottle without anyone noticing your actions.

Why does this work?

Watch the air column in the diver as you squeeze the bottle. What happens to the size of the air column when the diver sinks?

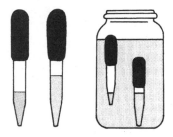

When you squeeze the bottle, the pressure in the bottle increases. The air column will get shorter as more water forces its way into the diver and makes it heavier. Thus, if you put too much water in the diver at the very beginning, the diver will sink and stay down.

Did you ever watch a water snail sink and float in an aquarium? For millions of years, water snails have used the same principle as our diver to sink or float. Some fish use their balloon-shaped air bladders to sink or float.

Pretend you are designing a submarine. You have attached a "float tank" to the submarine so that the volume of air can be controlled by pushing a button. Increasing the volume of air causes the submarine to rise. Decreasing the volume of air causes the submarine to sink.

How Many Paper Clips Can a Cup Hold?

For this activity, you need:

○ a glass
○ water
○ a box of paper clips

To do this activity:

Fill the glass with cold water until the water level just reaches the rim of the glass. Show the glass to your friends. Let them predict how many paper clips you can drop in the glass until the water overflows. Record their predictions. Let your friends count out loud as you drop each paper clip carefully into the glass. Continue until the water overflows. To everybody's surprise, the glass will hold almost the full box of paper clips.

See whose prediction is nearest to the correct number of paper clips. Ask the person to explain his or her reasoning.

You can do the same activity by adding water drops to the glass with an eyedropper. Ask your friends to predict how many water drops can be added before the water overflows. Begin to add water drops by squeezing the eyedropper.

From *Showy Science* published by GoodYearBooks. Copyright ©1994 by Hy Kim.

How can the glass hold so many paper clips or water drops?

The water level increases by amounts equal to the volume of each paper clip added to the water. If you observe the side view of the jar, the water level is rising higher than the rim of the jar. A special force allows the water to pile up in the shape of a small mound above the rim.

Water is made up of very small units of molecules. Each molecule is just like a tiny magnet with a positive end and a negative end. The positive end of one molecule attracts the negative end of another molecule. Because of this, all the molecules in the glass are attracted to each other. This attracting force is called *cohesion*. This is the reason raindrops are shaped like spheres. This force explains many attributes of water. The next activity also explores this cohesive force.

A Water Dropping Contest

This activity is most fun when you do it in teams of two.

For this activity, each team needs:

○ one penny
○ an eyedropper
○ a small cup of water
○ a piece of paper towel

To do this activity:

Ask the teams how many drops of water they think they can put on a penny before the water slides off. Record the predictions on the chalkboard or a piece of paper. Two teams can win: the team that most closely predicts the number of drops that fall on the penny, and the team that places the most drops on the penny.

Have the teams place a penny on a piece of paper towel and drop water on the coin with the eyedropper. Count the drops until the water spills over on the paper towel. Record the number of drops of water next to the predicted numbers.

Determine the winners. The first thing the participants will say is that they didn't know so many drops of water could be piled on a penny. The side view will look like the illustration below as the water on the surface bulges at the rim.

Why does this happen?

The water molecules have an attraction for each other called cohesion. This attraction forms a bond at the surface called surface tension. Water on the surface will bulge above the rim as the molecules cling together. Gravity soon overcomes this force as the pile gets higher and the water spills over the side of the penny.

Floating Pins, Needles, and Paper Clips

Toothpicks, pencils, and many other light objects float. Do metals such as pins, needles, and paper clips float? You can show your friends that it is possible to make pins, needles, and paper clips "float" on top of a bowl of water.

For this activity, you need:

○ a bowl or a glass
○ water
○ a needle
○ a pin
○ a few paper clips

To do this activity:

Fill a bowl or glass to the top with cold water. Carefully place a needle on the surface of the water. If you are very careful, the needle will remain on the surface of the water.

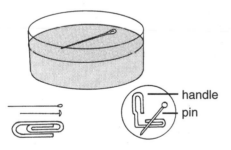

A separated paper clip (as illustrated in the circle above) is a handy item used to float the needle, pin, and paper clip. Lay a needle on the paper clip as shown in the circle. Gently place it on the surface of the water. Let some of your friends "float" the paper clips, too.

Why does this work?

Look closely at the floating metals. Notice that the surface seems pushed down under the needle. The surface also seems to be elastic. The activity, "How Many

Paper Clips Can a Cup Hold," introduced you to the concept of cohesion. Each water molecule acts like a small magnet that attracts other molecules, not only on the surface of the water but below the surface as well. This cohesive force on the surface of water is called *surface tension*. The surface tension is what causes the metal things to "float." A light object, such as your needle, simply rests on the surface film. This surface film can be broken or penetrated. The following activity demonstrates this clearly.

Sink the Paper Clip

For this activity, you need:

○ a bowl
○ a paper clip, pin or needle
○ a toothpick
○ a bar of soap

To do this activity:

Fill the bowl with water. Float a paper clip on the water's surface as you did in the previous activity. Scratch the soap with one end of the toothpick so that some soap remains on the end of the toothpick. Poke the water near the floating paper clip with the soapless end of the toothpick.

Nothing will happen to the paper clip. If you have an audience, announce that with your magic power, you can sink the paper clip by dipping the same toothpick. Poke the same spot of water with the soaped end of the toothpick. What happens to the paper clip? It sinks! (This may seem like magic to someone who does not know the reason.) Float another paper clip on the water's surface. Touch one area of the water with the bar of soap and watch what happens. The paper clip will push away to the opposite side of the soap, and then it will sink.

Why does this happen?

Soap is a chemical that weakens the cohesive force of water. Soap, therefore, breaks the surface tension.

From *Showy Science* published by GoodYearBooks. Copyright ©1994 by Hy Kim.

To do a similar activity:

Many fun activities can be done by breaking the surface tension of water with soap. Here's another one: Float a loop of string on a bowl of water. Touch the surface of water inside the loop with a bar of soap and watch what happens.

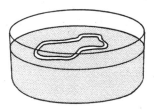

Instantly the loop will expand, forming a circle.

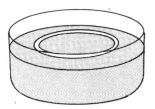

If you touch one corner of the water's surface with soap, the loop will be repelled in the opposite direction.

The Floating and Sinking Egg

You have a bottle containing water and an egg. Ask your friends whether the egg will float or sink in the water. Then place the egg in the water. The egg sinks. Now announce to your friends that you can make the egg float in the water. Remove it from the water. Concentrate on the egg, then replace it in the water. The egg floats!

For this activity, you need:

○ two identical jars with wide rims

○ an egg

○ salt

○ water

To do this activity:

First fill the two jars about 1/2 full of water. To one jar, add some salt and stir it thoroughly with a spoon. Place an egg in this jar of salt water. Keep adding salt until the egg floats. Wait a while until the salt water clears and appears identical to the plain water. Now the show begins!

Hide the jar of salt water in a convenient place so you can exchange it later for the jar of plain water. Show your friends the jar of plain water and an egg. Ask them to guess whether the egg will sink or float in the water.

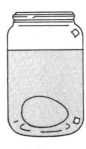 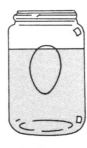

Have one of your friends place the egg in the water. It will sink. Tell them that you can float the egg. Take the egg out of the jar. Out of their sight, replace the jar with the one full of salt. Say some magic words. Place the egg in the water. It will float! If you cannot replace the jars without being seen, start the show with both jars visible. Ask them why the egg sinks in one jar and floats in the other. Demonstrate the activity for them.

Why does this work?

An egg is denser than tap water. In other words, an egg is heavier than an equal volume of water. Coins, nails, spoons, dishes, and other heavy objects sink in water for the same reason. However, if we add salt to the water until the solution is denser than the egg, the egg will float. (The results are the same if you use sugar instead of salt.)

A Straw Hydrometer

A hydrometer is an instrument that measures the density of a liquid. You can make a hydrometer simply by using a straw and a paper clip. It can be useful in many science activities.

For this activity, you need:

○ a drinking straw

○ a large paper clip (or three small ones)

   (To demonstrate the hydrometer, you will also need the two jars of water from the previous activity.)

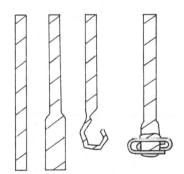

Flatten about 5 centimeters of one end of the plastic drinking straw with your fingers. Fold the flattened end three or four times as in the illustration. Clip the folded part with a large paper clip or three small paper clips. Now your hydrometer is complete.

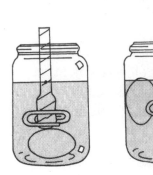

To test the hydrometer, drop it in tap water. Cut off the tip about 5 centimeters above the surface so it can balance better in the liquid. Mark the water level on the straw as shown above.

Now place the hydrometer in the salt water used in the previous activity. Mark the water level on the straw. Try using the homemade hydrometer to measure the density of liquids such as orange juice, milk, etc.

Why are the two marks different for tap water and salt water?

Salt water is more dense than tap water. Therefore, the salt water exerts greater pressure and pushes up more strongly. You may want to draw lines so that you can read them easily when you test the density of different liquids. You can also use the homemade hydrometer in the following activities.

Floating and Sinking Soft Drinks

For this activity, you need:

○ two unopened aluminum soft drink cans: one diet and the other regular
○ a container of water in which you can place the cans
○ masking tape

To do this activity:

First, be certain that the cans are made of aluminum. Then tape the labels with masking tape so that each can looks identical.

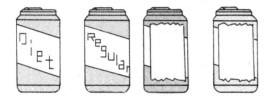

Now ask your friends to identify the diet soft drink and the regular soft drink. They are not allowed to open the cans! Write their names on the tape of the can they identified as diet. Ask the reason for their choice.

Show them which can is diet by conducting this simple, but scientific, experiment. Place both cans into the container of water. One can will sink and one will float. The floating one is the diet soft drink and the other is regular soft drink. To verify the fact, remove the covers from the labels. See who identified the cans correctly.

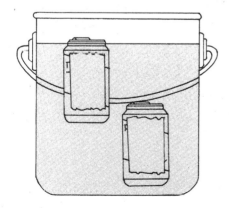

Why does the regular soft drink sink and the diet soft drink float?

The regular drink has lots of sugar, and the diet has none. The diet drink is sweetened with a much lighter compound. Therefore, the regular soft drink is much denser than the diet soft drink. The following activity will prove how much sugar there actually is in a can of soft drink.

How Much Sugar Is in a Can of Soft Drink?

How can you find out how much sugar is in a can of soft drink? None of your friends will have the answer to this question. But you can do an impressive activity that will tell you about how much sugar is dissolved in a can of soft drink.

For this activity, you need:

○ a homemade hydrometer
○ two cups large enough to hold a can of soft drink
○ a spoon
○ a bag of sugar

To do this activity:

Open a can of regular soft drink, and pour the drink into a cup. Leave it uncovered overnight so that when you work with the soft drink, there are no gas bubbles. Fill the other cup with tap water to the same level as the soft drink.

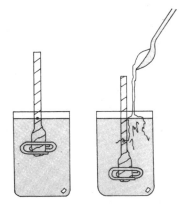

Place the hydrometer into the soft drink, and mark the level on the straw. Place the hydrometer into the tap water and mark the water level on the straw. Add a spoonful

From *Showy Science* published by GoodYearBooks. Copyright ©1994 by Hy Kim.

of sugar to the tap water, and stir the water. Count the number of spoonfuls you put in. Keep adding sugar until the mark on the hydrometer floats at the mark made by the soft drink. This means that the density of the two liquids is the same. Therefore, the amount of sugar you put into the tap water is equal to the amount of sugar in the soft drink. Are you surprised at how much sugar there is in a can of soft drink?

Why Does Warm Water Float and Cold Water Sink?

Ask your audience what will happen when warm water and cold water meet. Using one bottle of cold water with food coloring in it and one bottle of warm water, you can show that cold water flows under warm water. This activity will help you explain to your friends how some ocean currents are formed.

For this activity, you need:

- ○ a glass pop bottle
- ○ a jar with a mouth large enough to suspend the pop bottle in the jar
- ○ warm water
- ○ cold water
- ○ a Styrofoam cup
- ○ a small piece of paper
- ○ food coloring

To do this activity:

Remove any labels and clean off any glue on the bottle and jar. Place a Styrofoam cup in the mouth of the large-mouthed jar. Mark the cup about 1 centimeter above the rim of the bottle. Cut off the cup at the mark. Cut off the bottom part of the cup also.

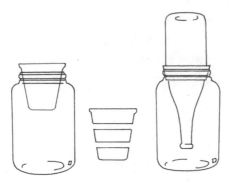

Now you have a Styrofoam washer. Later, you will place this washer between the bottle and the jar.

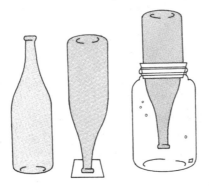

Fill the pop bottle to the top with cold water. Add some food coloring to the water and shake. Fill the jar to the top with warm water. Cover the opening of the pop bottle with a small piece of paper. Carefully turn the bottle upside down while holding the piece of paper over its mouth. Place the pop bottle through the washer and into the jar of water. Carefully, but firmly, grasp the bottle and jar and turn them upside-down. Observe what happens.

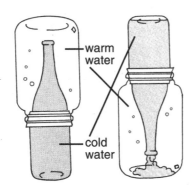

warm
water

cold
water

Nothing happens, as shown in the illustration above. Turn the two bottles upside-down again so the cold water bottle is on top. Watch this system for a while. The colored cold water will flow down through the warm water. The following is another demonstration of this principle.

From *Showy Science* published by GoodYearBooks. Copyright ©1994 by Hy Kim.

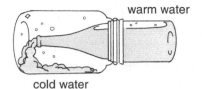

warm water

cold water

Refill the bottles with cold and warm water as you did in the previous activity. This time, turn the system on its side. Observe how the cold and warm water flow. You will clearly see that the colored cold water flows out of the pop bottle and sinks in the jar. On the other hand, the warm water will rise from the jar to the pop bottle and float on top of the cold water. This two-way movement will continue for a short time.

Why does this work?

Warm water molecules are more active and take up more space than cold water molecules. Therefore, one unit of warm water molecules is slightly lighter (less dense) than one unit of cold water molecules. Thus, cold water sinks and warm water rises when they meet. This movement is called a *convection current*.

Have you ever jumped into deep water during summer? Usually, deep water is cooler than surface water because of this convection current. In the same way, some parts of the earth are warmer than other parts. Ocean water near the equator is much warmer than water near the poles. Convection current is what powers ocean currents.

A Water Hourglass

An hourglass is an instrument used to measure a certain length of time. You do this by flipping over the hourglass and letting sand fall from the upper part to the lower part. An hourglass is specially designed and enclosed for just this purpose. This simple instrument is accurate in measuring a certain length of time.

For this activity, you need:

○ two glasses
○ a large container filled with water
○ rubber or plastic tubing
○ water
○ a small box or book

To do this activity:

Fill the two glasses a little more than halfway with water as shown below. Place the tubing in the container so that it is completely filled with water. Fold the tubing at the middle point, pinch it, then remove it. The water inside it will not flow out if you keep pinching the middle while lifting it up. Insert each end of the tubing into a glass of water. The water will remain in the tubing.

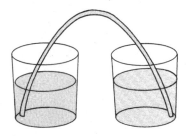

Now place one glass on a small box or book to raise it above the the other glass. This is illustrated below. Watch the water levels of both glasses.

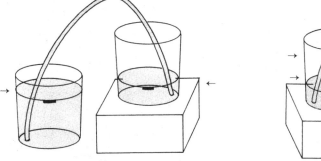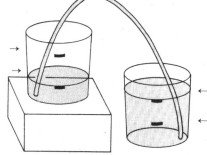

Water from the elevated glass will flow down to the other glass until the water levels are equal. Mark the water level on each glass.

From *Showy Science* published by GoodYearBooks. Copyright ©1994 by Hy Kim.

Now exchange the positions of the two glasses. Watch how the water levels change in both glasses. This indicates that water flows downward from the higher glass to the lower glass. Mark the new water level on each glass. By continually exchanging the position of the glasses, you can use this "hourglass" to measure time.

Use a watch with a second hand to measure the time it takes for the water to flow from the higher mark to the lower mark. You can control the length of time by using different-sized tubing, by changing the height of the book or boxes on which the glass is placed, or by pinching the tube with a clothespin. You can use this water hourglass in many activities that have a time limit such as making a move in a chess game or solving a problem in a timed test.

Why does the water flow from the higher level to the lower level?

When one side of the tubing is lower than the other, the weight of the water in the lower column is greater than that in the higher column. The greater weight draws water through the tubing from the higher side until the water levels are the same. This tubing system is called a *siphon*. A siphon is used in the next few activities.

An Automatic Smoking Machine

By making and using a smoking machine, you can demonstrate the effects of tobacco on a smoker's lungs. (This is a good science fair project.)

For this activity, you need:

○ an adult helper
○ two large identical bottles
○ a piece of clear plastic tubing (about 10 centimeters long) wide enough to hold a cigarette
○ about 70 centimeters of thin tubing
○ a white sponge cube
○ a pack of cigarettes

○ matches
○ rubber cement
○ a book or box
○ a pair of scissors

To do this activity:

As in the illustration below, make a hole in the center of the cap of a bottle. Place the piece of plastic tubing in the hole and secure it with rubber cement. The clear plastic tube is used as a bronchial tube to show nicotine contamination. Make a hole on one side of the sponge cube. Secure the sponge to the end of the clear plastic tubing that protrudes from the bottom of the cap. The sponge is a model of a lung.

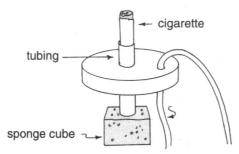

Make another hole in the cap, and insert one end of the thin tubing through the hole. This tubing should almost touch the bottom of the bottle when the cap is placed on the bottle. Seal the tubing to the cap with rubber cement. Fill the bottle with water, put the cap on, and tighten it.

With an adult's help, light a cigarette and place it in the clear plastic tube that is connected to the sponge. Place the system on a box as shown below. Use your mouth to draw water through the thin tubing. When water fills the tubing, collect it in the other bottle.

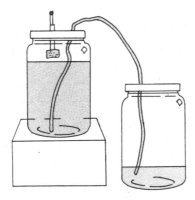

As water runs from the higher to the lower bottle, air will be drawn through the cigarette and will collect nicotine in the model lung. When all the water has been siphoned from the higher bottle, exchange the bottles so that water flow can continue.

If you keep the system running until it burns a pack of cigarettes, the model lung and bronchial tube will change into blackish, nicotine-contaminated bundles. The contaminated model of a lung will convince you and your friends of the harmful effects of smoking more forcefully than any lecture.

Climbing Water

Water flows downward because of gravity. However, you can show that water can also climb upward. This mysterious and very important concept is called *capillarity*. In this activity you can show a dramatic view of capillarity on a glass wall.

For this activity, you need:

○ a glass partially filled with water
○ a piece of plastic wrap or flexible plastic
○ a pair of scissors
○ food coloring (will aid in observing the climbing water)

To do this activity:

To set up the system, cut a piece of plastic wrap into a rectangular shape and fold it in a T-shape as shown below.

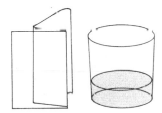

The height of the plastic wrap should be a little greater than the height of the glass. If you add some food coloring to the water in the glass, you can see the result more easily than in plain water. Insert the plastic wrap into the glass.

The illustration above shows the view when you look downward into the glass after the plastic is inserted. Notice that the gap between the glass and the front side of the plastic is gradually narrowed and then closed. If your structure does not look like the illustration, fold another piece of plastic. Watch how the water climbs the gap between the glass wall and the plastic. The climbing water will look like the illustration. If the gap between the glass and plastic is very narrow, the water will climb very high.

Why does this work?

Water molecules are attracted to some solids upon contact. As in the demonstration, the water is attracted more to a narrow gap between the solids rather than a wide one. This phenomenon is called *capillary action*.

Tear off a piece of paper towel and insert one end into the water as shown above. Watch the water climb up the strip. Try this with other materials such as fabric, rope, yarn, and tubing. Capillarity can be used in many interesting science activities.

A Cotton Wick Siphon and Water Clock

Without plastic or rubber tubings, you can show siphoning by using a piece of cotton fabric. This cotton wick siphon can be demonstrated in many creative ways. One of these ways, a water clock, is an ancient method of indicating time periods.

For this activity, you need:

○ a rectangular piece of cotton fabric like an old, cotton T-shirt (The fabric should be cut into a rectangular shape, 30 by 3 centimeters.)

○ one large water-filled bottle

○ a small empty container

To do this activity:

Roll the fabric into a cylindrical wick. Place one end of the wick into a water-filled bottle. Hang the other end of the wick out of the bottle as in the illustration. Place the small container underneath the outside end of the wick.

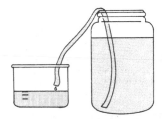

Watch what happens to the water at the end of the outside wick. If you wait for a while, the water will go up inside of the wick and come down the outside. If you wet the wick before placing it in the system, water drops will instantly drip from the end of the outside branch of the wick. On the wall of the small bottle, draw lines every elapsed hour. By doing this, you can measure how many hours have passed.

Why does this work?

Water goes up inside the wick by capillary action. As the water molecules reach the bend at the top of the wick, gravity and capillarity help the water run down the wick. As the wick becomes wet, the water is more quickly pulled by gravity. The wick acts as a cotton tube through which water travels in the same way as the rubber tubing in the earlier activity.

From *Showy Science* published by GoodYearBooks. Copyright © 1994 by Hy Kim.

Climbing Color Bands

Draw a black line on a piece of paper with a marker. Ask your friends to predict whether the black color is really black or a mixture of other colors. If they think it is a mixture, ask them how they would find out what colors are mixed to make black. By doing a simple experiment, you can show them that a black marker is really a mixture of different colors.

For this activity, you need:

○ paper towels or a coffee filter
○ a black felt-tip pen or marker (not permanent)
○ a pencil or drinking straw
○ a glass of water

To do this activity:

Fill the glass about two centimeters deep with water.

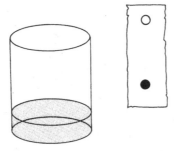

Cut a paper towel (or coffee filter) into a rectangular strip about 20 centimeters long. Make a dot with a black marker or felt-tip pen on the strip so that the dot is about 2 centimeters from one end. Suspend the strip by a pencil or a drinking straw as shown in the next illustration so that the dot is about one centimeter above the water. Watch what happens to the dot.

The black dot will change into bands of different colors. The marker or pen company used these colors to mix the black ink. By the same method, you can analyze some other colors to determine whether the color is made of a mixture of other colors.

From *Showy Science* published by GoodYearBooks. Copyright ©1994 by Hy Kim.

Why does this happen?

As the water climbs the paper strip by capillarity and reaches the dot, the pigments of the dot's ink dissolve into the water. If the color of the dot is a mixture of many other pigments, each material of the pigment may dissolve at a different rate. As the water moves up the paper towel strip, it will carry the dissolved pigments. At a certain point, the water will evaporate, leaving the pigments on the strip. As a result, you will see separated color bands. This is called a *chromatogram*.

A light pigment that has smaller molecules and dissolves in water quickly will be carried further up the column. A heavy pigment that has larger molcules and dissolves slowly will be carried a short distance.

By using the chromatogram, you may be able to find out which colors the marker company mixed to make black, orange, green, or any other color.

You can create many colors by mixing primary colors. The primary pigments are magenta, cyan, and yellow. By using a simple technique called *chromatography*, you can just as easily separate the primary colors from a mixed color. "Chroma" means color, and "graphy" means recording activity.

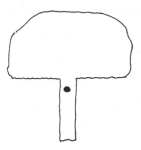

Instead of suspending the paper towel strips by the pencil, you can cut the paper towel in the shape illustrated. Secure the towel over the rim of the glass with tape.

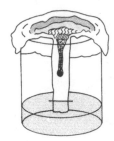

Make a dot with a marker located about 1 centimeter above the water. Observe the bands of colors that will form a rainbow on the paper towel.

Analyzing the Pigments in Green Leaves and Flowers

The color of leaves changes in autumn. As cold weather approaches, some leaves turn yellow or red. Why is this? By doing a simple chromatogram experiment, you can show your friends the scientific reasons why green leaves change.

For this activity, you need:

- ○ an adult helper
- ○ leaves
- ○ flower petals
- ○ rubbing alcohol
- ○ a pan
- ○ water
- ○ a heating device such as a hot plate
- ○ a paper towel
- ○ a glass
- ○ a pencil

From *Showy Science* published by GoodYearBooks. Copyright ©1994 by Hy Kim.

To do this activity:

Shred the leaves and petals and press them to the bottom of the glass. Pour in some rubbing alcohol. Place the glass in a pan filled with water as shown below. Ask an adult to help you heat it on the hot plate. The alcohol will boil at about 80° Celsius. The water will not boil until the temperature reaches 100° Celsius. You may have to open a window so that the odor of alcohol will dissipate.

CAUTION: DO NOT ALLOW FIRE NEAR THE ALCOHOL VAPOR. ALCOHOL IS HIGHLY FLAMMMABLE.

While you watch the boiling alcohol, the colors of the flower petals and leaves will dissolve in the alcohol. This leaves the petals and leaves colorless. At this point, turn off the heater and have the adult take the bottle out of the pan for you.

Remove the shredded leaves and observe them. What do you see?

Next, cut a strip of paper towel and suspend it as shown. You will create a chromatogram. Separate the greenish juice into a few glasses and let some of your friends make chromatograms also. The color bands may look different depending on the leaves and the flower petals you placed in the alcohol.

Why do different leaves produce different colors?

Some leaves have green chlorophyll and yellow pigments. Others have green chlorophyll and red pigments. Plants do not produce chlorophyll as the cold season approaches. Therefore, the green color fades somewhat. The yellow or red pigments can then be seen in the leaves. Try making chromatograms by using leaves from various plants such as the purple eggplant, maple tree, or dogwood.

Growing Large Salt Crystals

You can grow a crystal large enough for competition.

For this activity, you need:

- ○ an adult helper
- ○ salt
- ○ a glass of water
- ○ a paper clip or nail
- ○ string
- ○ a pencil

To do this activity:

Keep adding salt to a glass of water and stirring it until no more salt can be dissolved in the water. Tie a paper clip or a nail to a string and suspend it in the salt water by tying the other end of the string to a pencil as shown below.

Place the glass in an undisturbed, warm place. As the water evaporates, the salt will form crystals where the paper clip or nail is attached to the string. In this manner, you can slowly grow very small crystals. If you are in a crystal-growing contest, you will not win this way!

To grow a large crystal in a short period of time, you have to do more. In addition to the supplies in the last activity, you also need a pan, a heating device, and a cloth.

First, boil a glass of water in a pan while adding lots of salt; stir the water well. You can dissolve much more salt in boiling water than you can in cold water. Add salt until some of it floats on the water's surface. Now filter the water through a cloth into a glass. Suspend a string with a paper clip as you did in the previous activity. As the hot water cools down, salt crystals will form on the string and the paper clip very quickly, as shown in the illustration below.

To grow a large crystal, take the string out of the water. Remove all of the crystals except a large one. Then cut off the paper clip, and suspend the crystal in the water by the string. Within a few days, the crystal will grow and more small crystals will form. To grow an even larger crystal, repeat the process: boil water and dissolve lots of salt in it. Replace the old water with filtered boiling water. Now take out the string, remove the small crystals, leave one large crystal, and then suspend the crystal in the hot water. If you repeat the process several times, you can make a really large crystal in a short period of time.

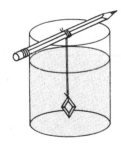

How does a crystal form?

As the salt dissolves in the water, the salt molecules separate into sodium and chloride ions. When the water evaporates, the sodium and chloride ions recombine into salt molecules in a cubical pattern. As the water evaporates, more salt molecules are added, thereby causing the crystal to grow.

Ice Power

Can you or your friends predict what will happen when you freeze a bottle of water. This activity shows what happens and why.

For this activity, you need:

○ a glass pop bottle
○ a Ziploc© bag
○ water

To do this activity:

Fill a glass pop bottle with cold water and seal it with its cap. Put the bottle in a Ziploc© bag, and place it in the freezer for a day or two. Ask your friends to predict what will happen and to explain their reasoning.

When one or two days have passed, take the bottle out of the freezer, and observe what happened.

The bottle will be shattered, just as the illustration above shows.

Why does the freezing water shatter the bottle?

When water freezes, the volume of the water increases. (You might compare this to a kernel of corn that increases in size when popped.) At room temperature, we know that water molecules attract each other, forming a liquid. As many experiments show us, water normally expands when it is heated and contracts when it is cooled.

From *Showy Science* published by GoodYearBooks. Copyright ©1994 by Hy Kim.

However, when the temperature goes below 4° Celsius, the volume of the water increases. When the temperature reaches the freezing point, the water molecules attract each other in a crystal pattern that leaves many empty spaces between the molecules.

As a result, the increased volume breaks the bottle. This ice power can be seen in everyday situations. A cooling system in a car can burst if its owner uses tap water in the winter instead of antifreeze. Ice power can expand potholes in the pavement and can even break rocks when water freezes in holes and cracks. What other examples of ice power can you imagine?

Ice Cream Shake-Up

Did you ever make ice cream? This activity is excellent for a whole classroom of students, or a party with many participants. Each participant can make his or her own ice cream.

For a group of ten to twelve participants, you need:
- 1 cup of sugar
- 2 cups of half and half
- 1 teaspoon of vanilla
- 1/4 teaspoon of salt
- 3 cups of milk

You will also need:
- salt (rock salt is better, but table salt will do just fine)
- pint and gallon freezer bags
- ice
- a large container for mixing up the ingredients

To make the ice cream:

Let some of the participants mix up the ingredients in a container. Identify each type of matter as a solid, liquid, or gas.

Now divide the participants into groups of two and give each group a one-gallon bag and a one-pint bag containing one cup of mixture. Seal the pint bag.

Have each group fill one-half of their gallon bag with crushed ice. Add one-fourth cup of salt. Place the pint bag inside the gallon bag, seal the bag, and have the participant shake up the bag. Each participant should shake the bag for about three minutes. Partners should share the shaking activities. Have them check the mixture in the pint bag every minute. Eventually they will discover that the mixture has changed into ice cream! Now have an ice cream party.

Why does it work?

Water freezes at 0° Celsius. Salt in the crushed ice lowers the freezing point of ice, causing it to melt. As the ice melts, it takes heat from the mixture in the pint bag. Even though the freezing point of the mixture is lower than the freezing point of water, the mixture freezes and becomes ice cream. Shaking the bag mixes the ice and salt in the gallon bag and keeps the pint bag mixture from forming into an ice block.

Ice Puzzle

This is a very simple and well-known science puzzle for individuals and small groups.

For this activity, you need:

- ○ a glass
- ○ water
- ○ ice cubes

Fill the glass half full with cold water. Put in a few ice cubes. The ice cubes will float. Do not let the ice cubes touch the bottom of the glass.

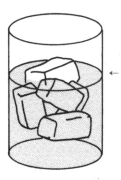

Ask your friends to predict whether the water level in the glass is going to increase or decrease as the ice melts. Have them explain the reasons for their predictions. Place a mark on the glass at the water level so that they can see if the level changes as the ice melts.

From *Showy Science* published by GoodYearBooks. Copyright ©1994 by Hy Kim.

What happens to the water level?

It does not change! When water freezes, the volume increases as in the "Ice Power" activity. When the ice melts, the volume decreases. The weight and mass of the water are the same whether solid or liquid. When an object floats in water, it displaces an amount of water equal to its weight. Therefore, the water level is constant before and after the ice is melted.

Picking Up an Ice Cube With a Toothpick

Ask your friends to pick up an ice cube with a single toothpick. They will struggle without success. You can pick up an ice cube with a toothpick in a magical way.

For this activity, you need:

○ ice cubes
○ toothpicks
○ salt

To do this activity:

Give an ice cube and a toothpick to each of your friends. Let them place the ice cube on a piece of paper. Then ask them to lift up the ice cube using only a toothpick. They will try many different ways to lift it, but they probably will not succeed. Ask one volunteer to help you. Now you can show them your scientific way to lift the ice cube.

Place a toothpick on an ice cube, as in the illustration, so that you can grasp one end of the toothpick. Sprinkle a pinch of salt along the ice cube over the toothpick, pretending you are placing some magical powder on the ice cube. Count to 30. Lift up the ice cube using the toothpick handle. The ice cube will be frozen to the toothpick! Next time, substitute a string, and the same magic will happen.

Why does this happen?

This activity works because of the same principle explained in "Ice Cream Shake-Up."

From *Showy Science* published by GoodYearBooks. Copyright ©1994 by Hy Kim.

ACTIVITIES FOR
EXPLORING
ANIMALS

A Pop Bottle Aquarium

¡S!

With a two-liter pop bottle, you can make a self-supporting aquarium to house many small pond animals. The aquarium looks like a magic world! Many pond animals like snails, scuds, water fleas, ostracods, paramecia, and others can be seen without a microscope. This little mini-world runs on its own much like earth.

For this activity, you need:

- ○ an adult helper
- ○ a two-liter pop bottle
- ○ a paper towel
- ○ paint remover, oil, or gasoline
- ○ hot water
- ○ a pair of scissors

To do this activity:

Remove the label from the bottle. Ask an adult to wash away the glue stain with a paper towel soaked in paint remover, oil, or gasoline. (Be very careful not to expose the soaked paper towel or any of these solvents to fire!) As shown in the next illustration, separate the black bottom from the bottle. To do this, fill the bottle with hot water. Wait until the glue that fastens the two parts softens, and then twist the black bottom off.

From *Showy Science* published by GoodYearBooks. Copyright ©1994 by Hy Kim.

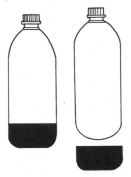

Use the scissors to cut away two sides of the black bottom to form a stand for the aquarium as shown below.

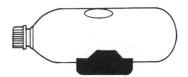

Now you are ready to bring the mini-world to the aquarium. You can use this aquarium in many creative ways. The following activities offer you a few ideas.

Small Animals in the Pond Water

The location and time in which you collect pond water for the aquarium is very important; both help maximize the number of small animals you trap. The animals are wise enough not to congregate in open water where many of their predators can find them. You have to search in a shallow edge of the pond near lots of dead leaves, decaying materials, and plants. At night, fish can't see the small animals. Therefore, you may have a better chance of collecting many small animals after sunset.

For this activity, you need:

- ○ a pop bottle aquarium
- ○ a paper cup
- ○ pond water that contains bottom dirt, small dead leaves, and some green filamentous algae (greenish bundles with fine threadlike plants)

To do this activity:

Use a paper cup to collect the pond water. Pour the pond water into the aquarium until it is half full. Screw the cap onto the bottle. You are ready to set the aquarium in your room or classroom and observe.

Place the aquarium on its stand on a windowsill where it is warm but not in direct sunlight.

The sediment will settle and the dirty water will clear in about an hour. You will probably see many unusual small "monsters" moving around inside. Does anything in your aquarium look like the animals in the illustration on the next page?

From *Showy Science* published by GoodYearBooks. Copyright ©1994 by Hy Kim.

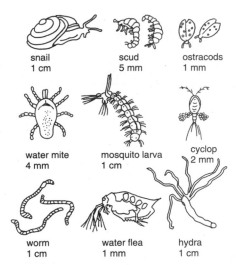

snail
1 cm

scud
5 mm

ostracods
1 mm

water mite
4 mm

mosquito larva
1 cm

cyclop
2 mm

worm
1 cm

water flea
1 mm

hydra
1 cm

If you are very lucky, you may find some large animals in the water, such as tadpoles, crayfish, water beetles, a mayfly nymph, small fish, and leeches.

After you set up the aquarium, you can spend hours observing the creatures of the mini-world: dashing scuds, wriggling mosquito larvae, hunting hydra, circling water fleas, dashing cyclop, scum-gobbling snails, swimming ostracods that look like cyclops, and wiggling small worms.

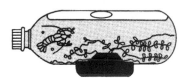

If you catch a crayfish, you can raise it in a pop bottle aquarium. Cut a hole in the top of the aquarium. Crayfish love to eat meat crumbs. You can even build a rock shelter for your crayfish.

A Snail Aquarium

Which of these three aquaria provides the healthiest environment for the living things in it? Why? Do this next activity to find out the answer.

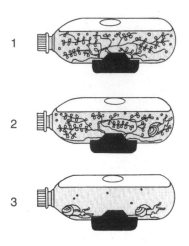

For this activity, you need:

○ three pop bottle aquaria
○ tap water or pond water
○ sand
○ three pond snails
○ water plants such as hornwort or water
   weed, or filamentous green algae

To do this activity:

Make three pop bottle aquaria. Fill each aquarium about two-thirds full with day-old tap water or clear pond water. Now add some sand.

Collect three pond snails and some water plants. If water plants are not available, you can find some filamentous green algae in a pond.

As shown in the illustrations, place a water plant branch or a bundle of washed algae in the first aquarium, one branch or a bundle of washed algae and one snail in the second aquarium, and two snails in the third aquarium.

Place the aquaria in indirect sunlight. Predict which aquarium will be best for the living things in it. (This kind of prediction is called a *hypothesis*.) Observe the living things in the aquaria for one month. Was your prediction correct?

From *Showy Science* published by GoodYearBooks. Copyright ©1994 by Hy Kim.

Which aquarium provides the healthiest environment?

The aquarium with the snail and plants will do very well. The green plants produce food and oxygen for the snail. Snails produce body wastes. (You may see the snails' solid body wastes in the aquarium!) Plants use some minerals and nitrates from these body wastes. Snails also produce carbon dioxide which is used by plants to make food. Some snails may even lay eggs in the aquarium!

Without green plants, snails do not have a source of food and oxygen. However, they can live for a few months in the aquarium because they may use algae or some other invisible source of food in the aquarium. Sometimes they go into a dormant stage under the sand.

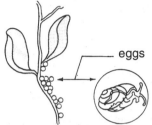

eggs

You may find a patch of snail eggs fastened to the wall of the aquarium or to the stem of a water plant. Snail eggs are fascinating to see through a microscope. The transparent shells of the embryo allow you to see the development of its organs. You can even watch its heart beat.

Do you think snails will overpopulate the aquarium in a few years? You may want to conduct a long-term experiment to find out.

Duckweed Farm

Duckweed is a free-floating freshwater plant that can be found on the quiet waters of marshes, ponds, lakes, and slow-moving streams. They are shaped like a clover but are much smaller in size.

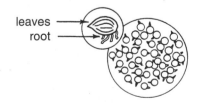

leaves
root

Duckweed is about one-half centimeter in length. Often, duckweed covers the surface of a whole marsh in the growing season. Ducks like to eat it, which explains its name. One good thing about duckweed is that under the right conditions, it multiplies very rapidly without increasing in size.

You may obtain duckweed from its natural habitat such as a marsh near your home. It is also available from local pet shops that sell aquarium supplies. One challenging contest is growing duckweed.

For this activity, you need:

○ a group of friends, divided into smaller groups
○ ten duckweeds per group
○ one pop bottle aquarium per group

To do this activity:

Announce that each group will be given ten duckweeds. They must grow the duckweed in an aquarium for a certain period of time. Encourage the groups to experiment to find the best conditions under which duckweed grows. Springtime is the best season to try this project. At the end of the experiment, count the number of duckweeds grown by each group to determine the winner. Have the winning group tell what they did to get their results.

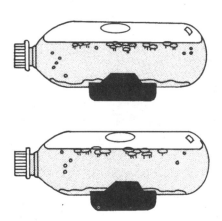

From *Showy Science* published by GoodYearBooks. Copyright ©1994 by Hy Kim.

A Demonstration of Eutrophication

Did you ever see a pond of smelly, muddy water full of dead fish? Sometimes, green plants called algae cause a pond condition called *eutrophication*. You can experiment with eutrophication in a pop bottle.

For this activity, you need:

○ a two-liter pop bottle

○ pond water

○ one cup of silt

○ a bundle of filamentous algae

○ plant food or fertilizer

To do this activity:

Fill the pop bottle almost to the top with pond water. Add the cup of silt from the bottom of the pond, a bundle of filamentous algae, and a small amount of plant food or fertilizer. Place the bottle on a windowsill where it can receive plenty of direct sunshine. Observe the bottle for a couple of weeks.

What happens in the bottle?

The algae will grow rapidly. Its bundle will become thicker and bigger. Excess nitrates, phosphorus, carbon dioxide, and direct sunlight will make the algae bloom. As the algae bundle gets thicker, the algae underneath and inside the bundle will die due to lack of sunlight. The decayed bacteria that feeds on the dead algae will multiply, using up the oxygen. Lack of oxygen will kill many small animals, including some bacteria. The water will become smelly and muddy, and the whole aquarium community will collapse. This is eutrophication.

Eutrophication may occur in a pond when an excess of fertilizer from a nearby farm washes into the pond, providing nitrates and phosphorus to the algae. Eutrophication could occur in any of your aquaria. One way to prevent it is to control the light source. Do this by placing the aquarium in a shady place, changing to smaller bulbs, or putting your light on a timer.

An Aquarium for Mosquito Fish

A mosquito fish is one of the smallest fish in most aquaria. It is known to be free from "the Ich," a disease in fish. You can tell if a fish has this disease if you can see little white spots on it. This symptom indicates the fish is infected by a parasitic protozoan known as *Ichthyophthrius*, also known as "ich."

Mosquito fish are abundant in almost all ponds and marshes in the United States. They are small, hardy fish that give live birth to their young.

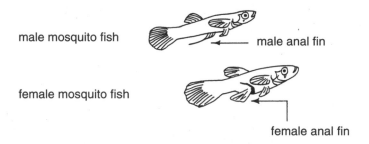

male mosquito fish — male anal fin

female mosquito fish — female anal fin

A mosquito fish is a type of minnow. The fully grown female measures about 3 centimeters in length. The male is smaller than the female. A male's anal fin is stick-shaped as shown above. A female's anal fin is round. The anal fins are clear signs to distinguish the male from the female.

From *Showy Science* published by GoodYearBooks. Copyright ©1994 by Hy Kim.

A pregnant female is easily identifiable because her tummy is full. When the black mark on her tummy grows, she is near to giving birth. You can obtain mosquito fish by buying them from a pet shop or by catching them in their natural habitat.

For this activity, you need:

- ❍ a pop bottle aquarium
- ❍ pond water (or a mixture of half pond water and tap water that has been aged for 6 hours in an open container)
- ❍ sand
- ❍ gravel
- ❍ green water plants (such as hornwort, water weed, or filamentous algae)
- ❍ two pond snails
- ❍ two mosquito fish in the aquarium

To do this activity:

Fill a pop bottle aquarium about two-thirds full with pond water. Place some sand, some gravel, green water plants, two pond snails, and two mosquito fish in the aquarium. Place the aquarium in indirect light. Feed the fish with any fish food. Now your aquarium is ready for the next exercise.

Fish and Green Plants

The illustration below shows two aquaria, one with green plants and the other without green plants. Which aquarium will be healthier for the fish? Why? How can you prove that your hypothesis is right?

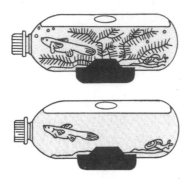

For this activity, you need:

○ two pop bottle aquaria
○ pond water
○ 4 fish
○ green plants

To do this activity:

Make two aquaria. Put one fish and some water plants into one aquarium. Put only fish into the other aquarium. You should make a small hole on top of each aquarium. This hole is not for air exchange, but for pressure control when the temperature changes. Watch how the fish behave.

What happens in the aquaria?

You will probably observe the same result as you did with in the activity, "A Snail Aquarium."

How Does Cold Water Affect Fish?

For this activity, you need:

- ○ two pop bottle aquaria
- ○ water
- ○ fish
- ○ ice cubes

To do this activity:

Make two aquaria, and fill them with water and fish. Place two or three ice cubes in one of the aquaria. Watch the fish's movement in both aquaria. Observe the frequency of their mouth movements per minute.

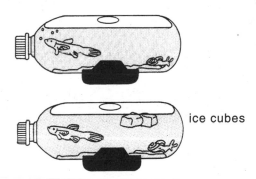

ice cubes

What is happening in the aquaria?

As the ice melts and cools the water temperature, the movement of the fish will slow down. This is because the fish's body temperature changes with the water temperature. The body temperatures of snakes and frogs also change with the temperature of their surroundings. These animals are called *cold-blooded*.

Do you know why a fish always moves its mouth? It takes in water through its mouth and pumps the water out through its gills. Gills are openings on the side of a fish's head. By this method, they take in oxygen that has dissolved in water, and they release carbon dioxide. You can compare this to the way we inhale and exhale air. Notice how the fish's breathing rate slows as the temperature drops.

Separating the Babies

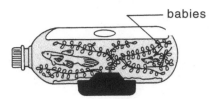

babies

You may be lucky enough to see a female mosquito fish give birth to her live young. She may have between five and fifteen babies in each litter. The newborn babies will move immediately after birth and hide themselves under plant leaves or gravel. In their natural habitat, the babies spread themselves over a wide area of pond water. In the aquarium, they cannot hide themselves very well, and the adult fish may eat them. Therefore, you have to separate them as soon as they are born.

Growing a Monarch Butterfly

How would you like to grow a monarch butterfly in your living room or classroom? Growing monarch butterflies is one of the most enjoyable science projects. It is amazing to watch the magical transformation of a seed-like egg into a tiny caterpillar; from a wiggly caterpillar into a chrysalis; and then from a chrysalis into a beautiful monarch butterfly.

For this activity, you need:

○ a monarch butterfly egg or a caterpillar (Read on for information on finding these.)

○ a bowl

○ water

○ a sponge

○ a wire cage

From *Showy Science* published by GoodYearBooks. Copyright ©1994 by Hy Kim.

To do this activity:

You can find monarch eggs and caterpillars in the spring or summer by taking a walk in a field where wild grasses grow. Identify a milkweed; it grows almost everywhere! In late fall, the plant seeds are blown out from the seed pot like dandelion seeds, as illustrated in the circle below.

Carefully examine the underside of each milkweed leaf. Monarch eggs are very difficult to identify; they are just white specks about the size of a pinhead. You will find a caterpillar more easily than an egg. When you have found an egg or caterpillar, break off the leaf on which it is attached or transplant the milkweed to a pot. Fill a small bowl with water and place a sponge in it. Insert the leaf into the wet sponge so that its stem is always wet.

Place this bowl in a wire cage. This cage, as shown below, is handy because the caterpillar will explore its space.

A caterpillar will hatch from the egg in about five days. At birth, the caterpillar will be about 2 millimeters long. It will have an off-white color with a tiny black dot on its head.

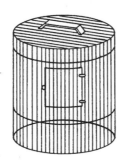

Caterpillars eat a lot. Provide fresh milkweed at all times. The baby caterpillar will grow rapidly, doubling its size in less than 24 hours.

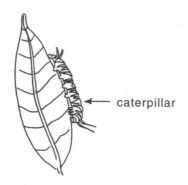

caterpillar

Within two weeks, it will multiply its original weight by 2,700 times. The caterpillar, or larva, will shed its skin five times as it grows. About fourteen days after hatching, the caterpillar will have grown to about 6 or 7 centimeters in length.

Fully grown, the monarch caterpillar will stop eating. It will crawl around, looking for a good place to begin the next stage of its life. The caterpillar finds a sheltered place on the milkweed, on the rim of the flower pot, or on the ceiling of the cage. There, it sheds its last skin. It then hangs upside down and spits out a silky substance, which it quickly pulls up over itself like a sleeping bag. By this process, the caterpillar is miraculously transformed into a blue-green chrysalis (pupa) studded with jewel-like gold specks.

The chrysalis will gradually become transparent during the next two weeks. Through the chrysalis, you can watch the colorful wings of the monarch butterfly developing. This entire process is called *metamorphosis*.

Cracks will start to appear across the chrysalis wall, and the beautiful monarch butterfly will emerge fully grown. The shedding of the chrysalis is called *molting*. The butterfly will then wait about an hour before it tries to fly away. Now you must take the cage outside and release the butterfly. Say goodbye to your departing friend.

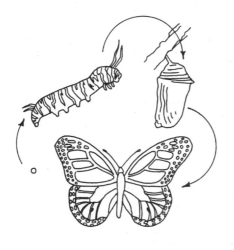

From *Showy Science* published by GoodYearBooks. Copyright ©1994 by Hy Kim.

More information about monarchs:

As the shorter days and cooler nights of late summer draw near, millions of North American monarchs fly south to regions like the California coast or south central Mexico. On these migratory routes, the butterflies travel some 2000 miles at altitudes of more than 3000 feet. Only 1 percent of these butterflies survives the winter to return north in the spring. Anticipating this, the butterflies lay their eggs on milkweed, which is plentiful almost everywhere.

Mosquito Aquarium

Some people dislike mosquitoes because they bite and carry disease-causing germs. In spite of the negatives, the mosquito is a very interesting insect to study, and it is easily obtained. If you make a mosquito aquarium, you can observe a mosquito's complete life cycle: egg to larva to pupa and finally to adult mosquito. You may enjoy watching the wriggling larvae and tumbling pupae in your mosquito aquarium.

For this activity, you need:

- ❍ a pop bottle aquarium
- ❍ a container of pond water for collecting mosquito larvae, OR
  a large container filled with water
- ❍ a large jar
- ❍ a nylon stocking
- ❍ a rubber band

To do this activity:

First, you must obtain mosquito larvae. You can do this by collecting pond water. However, there is an easier way to collect thousands of mosquito eggs and larvae in the spring, summer, and early fall. Fill a large container (such as a pail, a one-gallon jar, or a milk jug with its top cut off) with water. Place the container in a corner of a garage, under a tree or bush, or in a corner outside a school building. Wait a few weeks. Female mosquitoes will find the water and lay their eggs.

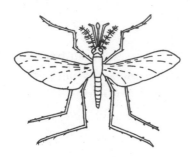

When you look for the wrigglers (larvae), you must watch the water carefully for a while. If you see only a few wrigglers, you have enough eggs and larvae in the container. A female mosquito lays up to 300 eggs at one time. Since the eggs are so small, you may not be able to see them without a microscope.

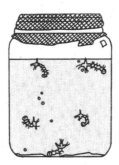

Pour the water from this container into a large jar so that it is half-full as shown above. A one-gallon pickle jar is ideal, but a pint-size jar will be fine. If the water is dirty, you can fill the remaining half of the jar with clear pond water. Cover the jar securely with an old nylon stocking by tying it with a rubber band. You do not want the mosquitoes to escape from the aquarium!

If you are making your mosquito aquarium at school, you can make at least ten more aquaria by using the same container of water, larvae, eggs, and pupae. Many female mosquitoes have probably laid eggs in the water at different times. If you watch the aquarium, you will discover that some of the pupae will change into adult mosquitoes at the same time that some of the larvae are hatching from eggs.

The constant movement of the larvae, pupae, and adult mosquitoes will attract your attention. Look carefully, and you will see the complete life cycle of a mosquito: egg, larvae, pupa, and adult.

From *Showy Science* published by GoodYearBooks. Copyright ©1994 by Hy Kim.

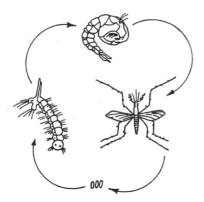

What will happen in the aquarium?

You may discover many things happening in your aquarium. All the larvae and pupae stick their tubes out of the water and stand still to breathe air. When they want to move, they wriggle their tails first, and their bodies follow. When they do move, they do so in a zigzag path as if to fool a fish. When you stand in front of the aquarium and cast your shadow over it, they dive deeply and quickly into the water. If you tap the jar, they immediately move to the bottom of the jar. The big jaws of the larvae nibble food, but the pupae don't have jaws. A pupa has two air trumpets that stick out of the surface of the water.

If a microscope is available, you can discover many wonders by viewing the parts of an egg, a larva, a pupa, and an adult. You may be fascinated by the delicate structure of the stick-like air tube on the eighth abdominal segment of a larva, a pair of respiratory trumpets on the first abdominal segment of a pupa, or the compound eyes of a pupa and an adult. You may also marvel at the digestive track of a larva, the difference between the antennae of male and female mosquitoes, the veins in a wing, and the pairs of swimming paddles attached to the last abdominal segment of a larva or pupa.

The distinguishing feature between the female and male common mosquito is the shape of the antennae. The antennae of the female have much less hair than that of the male. Because the female bites for blood, she uses her antennae, not her eyes or sense of smell, to detect the heat waves of warm-blooded animals. She locates her victim like a modern heat-seeking missile that homes in on a heat source and destroys the target. Human beings have recently built this kind of heat-seeking missile, but female mosquitoes have used their heat-seeking antennae for millions of years!

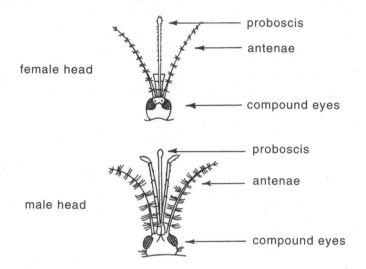

female head — proboscis
— antenae
— compound eyes

male head — proboscis
— antenae
— compound eyes

In contrast, the antennae of the male mosquito are quite hairy. These hairs vibrate to the high-pitched sounds made by the beating wings of a female mosquito. These vibrations guide the male to the female for mating. Scientists have found that male mosquitoes are attracted to a tuning fork that makes a hum similar to the hum of the female's wings.

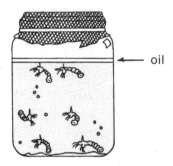

— oil

What will happen to the larvae and pupae if you add some cooking oil or a few drops of gasoline to the aquarium? They have to breathe by sticking their breathing tubes out of the water. If oil floats on the water and blocks their air tubes, they will die. Spreading oil on the water is one way to control the mosquito population.

From *Showy Science* published by GoodYearBooks. Copyright ©1994 by Hy Kim.

Mealworm Farm

Mealworms are good animals to study in classrooms. They are the gentle, active, harmless larva of grain beetles. The worms are about 2 to 3 centimeters long when they are fully grown. They are easy to obtain from local pet shops, who use them to feed chameleons, lizards, frogs, fish and other animals.

Mealworms are easy to keep. As they grow, they undergo a complete four-stage metamorphosis. Many science experiments can be done with them.

For this activity, you need:

- ○ a few hundred mealworms, which you can obtain from a local pet shop
- ○ a jar
- ○ corn bran or breakfast cereal
- ○ a potato

To do this activity:

Place some corn bran or breakfast cereal in a jar to provide food and shelter for the mealworms. Place a potato in the jar as in the illustration. The potato gives food and moisture to the mealworms. Put some mealworms in the jar.

The system will last for months, and you don't even have to add food or water. To observe the mealworms, stir their food occasionally and remove some mealworms. You will notice that the bran becomes powdery. There will be black specks of body waste mixed in the food. You may be able to observe that the mealworms have made a tunnel-like cavity in the potato by eating through it. You may even see sprouts of potato growing.

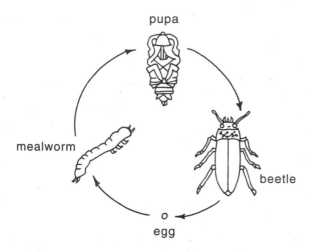

More information about mealworms:

You will probably see many old skins in the shelter because the mealworms shed their skins as they grow. Some mealworms change into immobile pupae, and some of the pupae change into beetles. Thus, the beetle has four distinct stages in its life cycle: egg, lava, pupa, and adult. Such a pattern of development is known as *complete metamorphosis.*

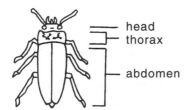

head
thorax
abdomen

Adult beetles are black. Their bodies have three parts: head, thorax, and abdomen. They have six legs. Antennae, eyes, and mouth are located on the head. They have wings, but they do not fly. After mating, the female lays many tiny white eggs. The eggs are attached to the their food, making them hard for you to identify.

The eggs will hatch in about one week. You may be able to see tiny threadlike larvae which shed and grow repeatedly until they reach 2 to 3 centimeters long.

The mature mealworms will change into pupae. At first their cases are white, but they gradually darken. You can see the developing insect's body parts through the case. Within a few weeks, the inactive pupae will develop into adult beetles.

For a similar activity:

Mealworm-growing contests with your classmates or with other friends are good science projects. Participants can grow them without much problem and observe the mealworms' whole life cycles within the shelter. While doing this project, participants may learn many variables in the mealworms' growth.

Divide your friends into small groups. Tell them that each group will be given between ten and twenty mealworms. Each group must grow the mealworms in a shelter for a certain period of time, searching for the best possible growing conditions. You should give the groups about six months to a year to complete the experiment. At the end of the time period, count the number of mealworms in each group's shelter to determine the winner. Have the winning team members tell how they grew their mealworms. You can then sell the mealworms to a pet shop!

Peeling an Eggshell

You can make an egg float in liquid, turn, sink, peel off its shell, and become an egg ball that bounces like a rubber ball. This simple activity is related to the chemical weathering that takes place on rocks on the hillside and also to the cavities in our teeth. This activity is an eye-catching, fun, and simple experiment.

For this activity, you need:

- a hard-boiled egg
- a jar
- vinegar

To do this activity:

Fill the jar with vinegar and place the hard-boiled egg inside with the cap loosely on the jar. Leave the jar in a place where it will not be disturbed. You can see many small bubbles form on the eggshell as soon as you place the egg in the vinegar.

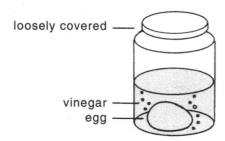

loosely covered

vinegar

egg

If you observe the egg for a while, some of the bubbles will grow and rise to the surface. At times, large bubbles will form on the bottom of the egg. The egg will move around because the egg and vinegar are denser than the bubbles. The egg will float as soon as enough bubbles are attached to it, and it will seem to be alive because the bubbles cause it to move.

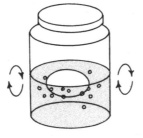

The vinegar will decompose the shell completely in one or two days. Wash the leathery egg, allow it to dry, and then try to bounce it. It will bounce like a ball!

126

From *Showy Science* published by GoodYearBooks. Copyright ©1994 by Hy Kim.

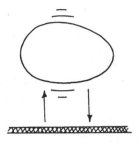

Why does this happen?

Several things happen to the eggshell during this experiment. In the acidic vinegar, the shell material ($CaCO_3$ or calcium carbonate) breaks down into two different materials: carbon dioxide gas bubbles (CO_2) which are released into the air, and lime (CaO or calcium oxide) which remains in the solution. The shell's appearance changes as a result of this chemical reaction. This process frequently occurs in nature, creating limestone caves. This chemical reaction also attacks your teeth. Now you know one reason why it is important to brush your teeth regularly.

Disappearing Chalk Pieces

For this activity, you need:

◯ a jar
◯ vinegar
◯ chalk pieces

To do this activity:

Drop tiny pieces of chalk in a jar of vinegar, and watch what happens. Before your eyes, the chalk will disappear, making bubbles. You can also drop tiny pieces of clam shells, snail shells, or limestone in the vinegar, and watch what happens. They all make bubbles.

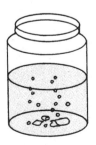

Why does this happen?

The bubbles occur because the materials in the vinegar are composed of the same materials as the eggshell—calcium carbonate. In nature, acid is present almost everywhere. Carbon dioxide in the air dissolves in rainwater and becomes carbonic acid. Smoke particles (which contain sulfur dioxide) added to rainwater forms acid rain. When dead plants or animals decompose, the decaying bacteria form acid. Acid water can create huge caves in limestone over a period of many years.

Our teeth are made of the same material as an eggshell. Cavities in our teeth are the result of a chemical weathering on the teeth. This occurs when decaying bacteria feed on food between our teeth. This bacteria produces acid, which causes the chemical weathering to take place.

If you soak a chicken bone in vinegar for a while, the bone becomes soft and bendable. The great portion of the chicken bone is made of the same material as the eggshell. These materials will disappear in the vinegar in a few days. After this treatment, you will find a very flexible chicken bone left with many small holes formerly occupied by calcium carbonate.

From *Showy Science* published by GoodYearBooks. Copyright ©1994 by Hy Kim.

The Swelling and Shrinking Egg

For this activity, you need:

○ two vinegar-peeled eggs
○ a jar of plain water
○ a jar of salt water

To do this activity:

Place one vinegar-peeled egg in a jar of plain water and another egg in a jar of salt water. As you can see below, one egg will shrink and the other will swell within a few hours. After the jars have been sitting for awhile, you may have difficulty telling which jar contains salt water and which jar contains plain water. Make a guess and explain why you guessed that way.

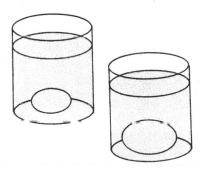

Why did one egg shrink and the other swell?

If you guessed that the jar in which the egg swelled contains plain water, you are right. Plain water, which has more water per unit volume than the egg white, goes through the soft membrane into the egg. This is how plants absorb water from the soil through their root hairs. The peeled egg is like a root hair that absorbs water. This process is called *osmosis*. It occurs because cells are lined up in plant roots and each cell has membranes that keep the cell materials in, but let water in and out through the membrane. The water from a swollen cell will go into the the next cell which has not been swollen. Through this relay osmosis, water gets to the top of branches of plants. The egg membrane represents the cell membrane.

In the other jar, water from the egg white, which has more concentrated water per unit than the salt water, moves out into the salt water through the membrane. As a result, the egg shrinks. For this same reason, a plant will wilt and die if you give it too much fertilizer, salt, or sugar. This process is called *plasmolysis*.

ACTIVITIES FOR
EXPLORING
PLANTS

A Self-Watering Bottle Planter

If you like to experiment with young plants and seedlings, a self-watering planter is for you. A bottle planter is a system that you can easily make with a two-liter pop bottle. It is convenient because it supplies water automatically. It is also handy; you can see the germinating process through the transparent plastic bottle.

For this activity, you need:

- ○ an adult helper
- ○ a two-liter pop bottle
- ○ a pair of scissors
- ○ paper towels
- ○ water
- ○ seeds

To do this activity:

Cut off the upper part of the bottle (about 11 or 12 centimeters from the top). An easy way to cut around the bottle neatly is to tie a string around it and use a marker to draw along the string. Ask an adult to make a horizontal slit with a sharp knife or scissor blade along the mark. (Slitting the bottle is easier if the cap is on the bottle tightly.) Start at the slit and cut along the mark with scissors.

From *Showy Science* published by GoodYearBooks. Copyright ©1994 by Hy Kim.

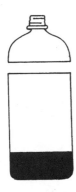

Take the upper portion of the bottle that you just removed. Invert it to make a funnel. Roll a piece of paper towel to make a column with a diameter of about 1/2 centimeter. Insert the paper towel column down through the mouth of the bottle as shown below. Now stuff some wet paper towels in the funnel around the column. (You can also use sand or dirt to fill the funnel.) Place some seeds in the funnel so that you can see them through the transparent plastic wall. Fill the bottom part of the bottle with water.

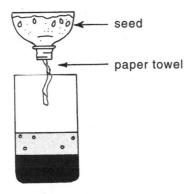

Place the "potting" funnel in the water as shown in the next illustration.

Adjust the paper towel column so that the paper towel touches the bottom of the container. Adjust the water level so that it almost reaches the mouth of the bottle. Your planter is finished! The paper towel column will bring water to the seeds until no more water is left in the container. (A glass canning jar is an even better water container than the lower part of the two-liter bottle. The funnel rests better on the glass bottle, and it is much easier to handle.)

How does this planter work?

Through capillary action, the paper towel column supplies water to the paper towel stuffing and seeds. Some water will evaporate through the upper part of the paper towel. If you want to keep in more moisture, you can cover the paper towel with a piece of aluminum foil or plastic wrap.

You can replace the wet paper towels with dirt or sand and the paper towel column with a cotton fabric wick. Once filled with water, this system is a perfect mini-flowerpot that does not require watering for several weeks.

You can use the bottle planter in many ways. In early spring, you can start growing garden vegetables. And you can discover the wonders and mysteries of a seed's germination process just by watching a seed develop into a young plant. The following activities are simple experiments you can do at home or at school.

How Does a Bean Change Into a Bean Plant?

Did you ever wonder how a seed changes into a mature plant? In this activity, you will see the changes a bean seed undergoes in the process of becoming a plant.

For this activity, you need:

○ a pop bottle planter
○ lima beans

To do this activity:

Make a bottle planter as you did in the last activity. Place two or three lima beans between the wet paper towels and the plastic wall of the bottle, as shown below.

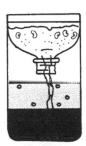

The column will bring water to the paper towels. You can observe the beans sprouting and growing through the transparent wall of the bottle. As the water penetrates the bean, the bean's coat swells and wrinkles. The whole bean swells into a larger size. Keep records and diagrams of your observations.

How does the bean grow?

The root (called a *primary root*) grows downward.

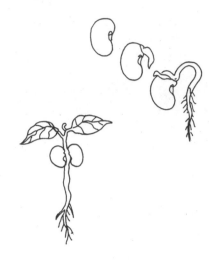

As the primary root grows, a stem will grow upward and pull the bean out of the paper towel. As the two *cotyledons* (which store food) of the bean open, its coat will drop, and leaves will develop on the tip of the stem. This is how a bean grows into a plant.

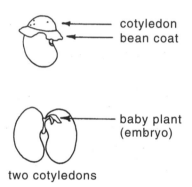

cotyledon
bean coat

baby plant
(embryo)

two cotyledons

It is easy to remove the bean coat because water has swollen the bean. If you expose the inside of a bean, you will find two cotyledons. Since it has two cotyledons, a bean is called a *dicotyledon.* You will find a baby plant between the two cotyledons. As a bean sprouts, food from the cotyledons changes into simple nutrients that can be used by and carried to the baby plant (called an *embryo*). This process is called *plant digestion*, and it is very similar to animal digestion. Simple nutrients are used by the embryo to grow.

A strong stem (called an *epicotyl*) grows, pushing itself out of the paper towel. It also pulls out the cotyledons. In a natural setting, the stem breaks the hard soil above it and pulls the cotyledons out of the soil. In this way, the stem protects the cotyledons. The stem can even push off rocks.

To do a similar activity:

Experiment with the stem's strength. Place a heavy coin on the stem when it emerges to the surface of the paper towel. Observe what happens.

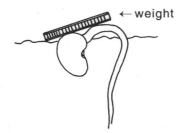

← weight

As the cotyledons are pulled out, the bean coat will tear and drop. The thick cotyledons will open, exposing the small leaves to the air. While its true leaves are developing, the cotyledons supply nutrients for the young plant. When the true leaves are fully developed and the young plant can make its own food, the cotyledons will wither and fall off the stem. A bean is a typical dicotyledon or dicot.

Sprouting Corn Seeds

This activity gives you the opportunity to observe a corn seed germinate.

For this activity, you need:

○ a pop bottle planter
○ a few corn seeds

To do this activity:

Make a bottle planter and place a few corn seeds in the system. Like the bean seed, water will swell the corn seed.

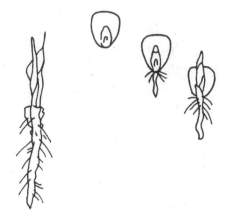

How does the corn grow?

A primary root with many root hairs will rupture the seed coat and grow. A young stem will appear. This stem is a cylindrical sheath called the *coleoptile* that protects the true leaves and stems inside it. The strong coleoptile breaks the hard soil and pushes off rocks as it grows. Its end opens so the true leaves and stems can grow in the air.

As the young plant grows, the cotyledon supplies food for the plant and then decays in the soil. The plant's leaves make food by combining water and carbon dioxide. It is on its way to becoming a fully independent plant.

If you open the seed coat, you will see only one cotyledon. *Mono* means "one" and corn is a typical *monocotyledon*, or *monocot*.

From *Showy Science* published by GoodYearBooks. Copyright ©1994 by Hy Kim.

What Is Phototropism?

For this activity, you need:

- ○ a pop bottle planter
- ○ seeds
- ○ a cardboard box

To do this activity:

Make a bottle planter and place some seeds in it. Place the planter in a cardboard box. Make a hole through which light can enter the side of the box. Have this opening face a window or a light. Watch how the new plants grow.

How does this happen?

Green plants tend to grow toward light. This tendency is called *phototropism* (*photo* means light). The plants grow toward the light because of plant growth hormones called *auxins*. Auxins collect in the cells on the dark side of the stem. The cells on the dark side then grow longer than the cells on the light side. As a result, the stem bends toward the light. Think of a way you can grow plants in a particular shape just by controlling the light source and its placement on the plants. You can be a tree tamer!

A Bag Greenhouse

You can make another kind of greenhouse to observe the sprouting of seedlings. A Ziploc© bag greenhouse is easy to make and convenient to use.

For this activity, you need:

- ○ a pop bottle planter
- ○ a Ziploc© bag
- ○ small seeds such as radish seeds
- ○ a wet piece of paper towel

To do this activity:

Lay the wet paper towel inside of the Ziploc© bag. Place the seeds on top of the paper towel. Blow into the bag to inflate it. Quickly seal the bag.

inflated bag

Place the greenhouse on a shaded windowsill or a dark place, and observe what happens to the seeds.

You can conduct many simple experiments in this type of greenhouse. By placing one greenhouse in the dark and another in a light place, you can experiment and find out in which place the seeds sprout faster. By placing one greenhouse in a warm place and one in a cold place, you can find out in which place the seeds sprout faster.

How does this greenhouse work?

Because the bag is sealed, the moisture remains in the bag and is used only by the seeds. Even though you exhale some carbon dioxide gas when you blow into the bag, the oxygen in the air, not the carbon dioxide, will be used in the sprouting seeds. The carbon dioxide gas will be used when the green leaves appear from the seeds.

From *Showy Science* published by GoodYearBooks. Copyright ©1994 by Hy Kim.

What Is Geotropism?

For this activity, you need:

○ a pop bottle planter

○ beans

To do this activity:

Make a bottle planter and place beans in it. Soon you will see the roots grow downward. Now change the positions of the root and the cotyledons as shown below.

Watch what happens to the roots. Soon you will see the upward roots grow down toward the earth.

Why does this happen?

This downward growth of the plant roots is called *geotropism*. (*Geo* means earth, and *tropism* is a natural tendency to react in a certain manner to stimuli). The plant growth hormone auxin is concentrated in the lower part of the root due to gravity. Auxin and another hormone make the roots grow downward.

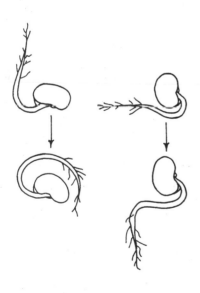

What Is Thigmotropism?

For this activity, you need:

○ a pop bottle planter
○ morning glory or garden pea seeds
○ a ruler that shows centimeters
○ a pencil or stick

To do this activity:

Make a bottle planter and plant some morning glory or garden pea seeds. After the seeds sprout and the stems grow about 5 centimeters tall, place a pencil or stick into the planter. The upper stem should touch the pencil or stick. Watch what happens to the stem.

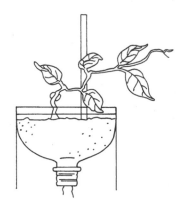

Morning glories and garden peas have winding structures that encircle sticks or fences.

From *Showy Science* published by GoodYearBooks. Copyright ©1994 by Hy Kim.

Showy Science

Why does this happen?

This response of growth to touch is called *thigmotropism*. It helps plants with weak stems grow upward. Without thigmotropism some plants could not compete with other tall plants for sunlight.

Sprouting Questions

For this activity, you need:

○ two pop bottle planters
○ seeds

To do this activity:

Place some seeds in both planters. Then place one bottle planter in a dark place, such as a closet or a cardboard box.

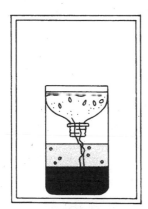

Place another planter in a sunny place. The temperature of the two places must be about equal. See which planter sprouts seeds first.

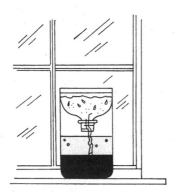

Which planter sprouts fastest under these conditions?

Usually, seeds sprout in a dark place just as fast as they do in a sunny place, sometimes faster. Sunlight is essential to green plants only after the seeds have sprouted. Baby plants use food stored in the seeds (cotyledons). Only after the leaves are developed do they need sunlight to make food for the growing plants. The chemical process of making food using sunlight is called *photosynthesis*.

For a similar activity, you need:

- ⭕ two pop bottle planters
- ⭕ seeds

To do this activity:

Make two planters. Place one in a warm place and the other in a cold place. (If you want to do this experiment in your room, remember that the floor is a little bit colder than the ceiling.) In which planter do the seeds sprout first?

Which planter sprouts fastest under these conditions?

As you probably guessed, seeds sprout more quickly in a warm place than in a cold place.

From *Showy Science* published by GoodYearBooks. Copyright ©1994 by Hy Kim.

Does Talking to a Plant Affect Its Growth?

For this activity, you need:

○ several pop bottle planters
○ seeds

To do this activity:

Make several planters. Wait until some of the young plants are grown. Then arrange the planters into two groups. Talk to one group of plants in a kind, complimentary manner. To the other group, use harsh words.

Conduct the experiment for a while, and observe any changes in the plants' growth. In order to get a fair result, control all other variables, such as the temperature and the amount of light. Make sure that you treat the plants equally in all other respects except the manner in which you speak to them.

What happens to the plants?

Different people may have different results. You can try turning on some rock music for one group of plants and some classical music to the other group. Observe the results.

In a Planter, Do Many Plants Do as Well as One Plant?

For this activity, you need:

○ two pop bottle planters, with soil instead of sand and with cotton wicks instead of paper towels

○ seeds

To do this activity:

Make two bottle planters. Use soil and cotton fabric wicks in place of paper towels. Plant several seeds in one planter. Plant one or two seeds (in case one seed does not sprout) in the other.

Do you think there is any difference in the length of time it takes the seeds to sprout? You will discover the results yourself. If the planter with two seeds sprouts two young plants, remove one plant. In order to get an accurate result, you have to control all other variables such as temperature, the amount and quality of soil, and the amount of light for the two planters.

What happens in the planters?

The seeds will sprout at the same time in both planters. However, many plants will not do as well in a single planter as one plant. In the planter with many plants, one or two will grow taller than the rest. Sometimes all of the plants will grow very thin and die. On the other hand, the solitary plant will grow big and healthy. This is mainly because the single plant does not have to compete for the limited resources in the planter.

Growing Bean Sprouts

You may have eaten bean sprouts in a Chinese restaurant or at home. Bean sprouts are not only good vegetables; they are also good subjects for study.

For this activity, you need:

- O a large paper or Styrofoam cup
- O a pin or nail
- O two bottles to suspend the cup
- O cotton fabric (like a cotton T-shirt or cheesecloth)
- O dried beans (such as mung beans or those available at a health food store)
- O water
- O a box

To do this activity:

Poke small holes in the bottom of the cup with a pin or nail. Place two layers of dried beans on the bottom of the cup. Cover the beans with a clean cotton fabric. Take another piece of cotton fabric, and roll it into a long column to make a wick.

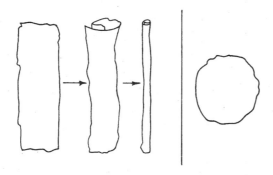

Place the cup inside the mouth of one of the bottles as in the illustration. Fill the other bottle to the top with water and place it on a box. Put one end of the wick in the water bottle and the other end on the cup's fabric layer.

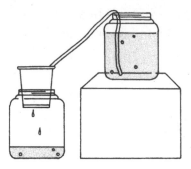

Place the sprouting system in a warm, dark place. Occasionally observe how it works. When water reaches the bottom of the cup, drain off the water. Add more water to the bottle.

As the beans sprout, they will push the cotton fabric cover. In about two weeks, depending on the temperature, you can harvest your homegrown bean sprouts.

As the sprouts grow, observe the germination processes. Measure the lengths of the sprouts. Experiment with the water-supplying device. Find the optimal temperature to grow plants quickly. Design a large-scale bean-sprouting factory. Research the nutritional values of the bean sprouts and find some recipes that call for bean sprouts.

Now you can cook your homegrown bean sprouts. They are great vegetables that have been used by Asian peoples for thousands of years, particularly in the winter season when other vegetables are scarce. If you have no idea how to prepare the sprouts, visit a local Chinese restaurant to get some ideas.

A Plant Self-Watering System

When your family goes on vacation, who waters the house plants while you are gone? Now, you can eliminate any worries by inventing a device that will water the house plants while you are away. Are the materials expensive? Is it difficult to make? No, not at all!

For this activity, you need:

- ○ an empty gallon milk jug
- ○ water
- ○ a potted plant
- ○ a cotton fabric wick

To do this activity:

As shown, cut off part of the milk jug's handle. Fill the jug with water until the water level reaches the cut.

Place the wick into the hole made by the cut so that one end of the wick touches the bottom of the jug. Bury the other end of the wick in the potting soil or place a small pebble on the wick to hold it in on top of the soil.

Check the system a day after you install it since at times excess water may collect in the saucer under the pot. Control the timing of the water flow by lifting or lowering the jug relative to the potting soil level. Another way to control the speed of water is by wrapping tape at various distances from the end of the wick that is on the soil. This ensures that the area touching the soil varies.

How does this work?

It works on the same principle as the wick siphon does in the "A Cotton Wick Siphon and Water Clock" activity. Through the capillary action, water spreads to all parts of the soil in the pot. If you watch the system and mark the jug for a long period of time, you will find out how long it takes to use one jug of water.

If you leave this device alone for a long time, the cotton wick will eventually rot. To prolong the life of the wick, you may insert it in a plastic tubing.

An Auto-Watering System for Potted Plants

This is another mysterious and innovative way to water potted plants.

For this activity, you need:

○ a gallon jar
○ water
○ a potted plant
○ a pan or rectangular dish
○ a toothpick
○ a wick
○ three pebbles

To do this activity:

Fill the gallon jar to the top with water. Cover the mouth of the jar with the pan. Flip the pan and jar over so that the jar is upside-down.

From *Showy Science* published by GoodYearBooks. Copyright ©1994 by Hy Kim.

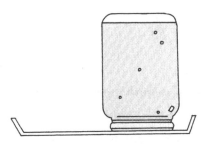

Lift up the jar slightly and insert a toothpick between the rim of the jar and the pan. A small amount of water will flow into the pan.

Remove the water-collecting dish from under the plant. Insert one end of the wick through a hole at the bottom of the pot. Leave the other end of the wick loose.

Place the pot in the pan as shown. Place three pebbles under the pot so its bottom does not touch the pan.

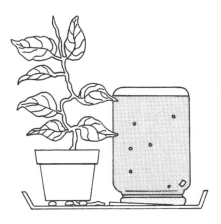

Water will reach the soil in the pot through the wick. A constant water level equal to the diameter of the toothpick will be maintained in the pan until all water in the jar is used.

Why doesn't the water in the jar flow out at one time?

A thin water layer seals off the rim of the jar, keeping air from going into the jar. When the water in the pan evaporates or is used by the plant, a slight gap forms between the rim and the bottom of the pan. Air goes into the jar through this gap, but an equal amount of water also flows out. This water flow stops when the water level reaches the rim of the jar and seals it again. Therefore, there is a constant shallow layer of water in the pan until all the water in the jar is gone.

Growing Plant Cuttings

There are many ways to grow new plants. You can grow them from seeds. You can grow them from the cuttings of stems, leaves, and roots of some adult plants. You can even grow them from roots, bulbs, and tubers. Common house plants such as the geranium, coleus, wandering Jew, African violet, peperomia, and the rex begonia can be grown from cuttings.

One of the most difficult tasks in growing new plants by this method is watering the cuttings for a long period of time. The self-watering system is handy because the system supplies adequate amounts of water for many weeks. You can make a bottle planter from different materials. Some samples are shown here.

 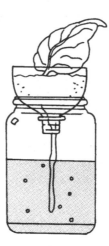

You've already made planters like those shown in the illustrations above. Now you can make the following planter, too.

For this activity, you need:

○ an empty wide-mouthed canning jar
○ a plastic or paper cup that can be suspended in the jar
○ a plastic straw
○ a piece of cotton fabric measuring 2 by 10 centimeters
○ a pair of scissors
○ water
○ sand
○ garden soil

To do this activity:

Make a hole in the center of the cup's bottom big enough for a drinking straw to fit through. Make several small holes around this hole to allow air to pass into the rooting area.

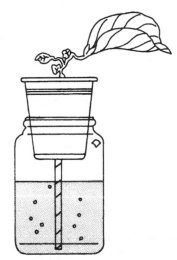

Cut the cotton fabric into a rectangle. Roll it into a cylindrical column and push it through the drinking straw. Slit one end of the drinking straw a few times and open it. Unroll one end of the fabric column as in the next illustration.

This is a wick through which water travels by capillary action. It is protected by the drinking straw. Insert the straw in the center hole of the cup with the exposed fabric up. Place the whole system in a bottle. Adjust the length of the straw so it is just above the bottom of the jar by cutting off the bottom end. Place a mixture of sand and garden soil in the cup. Fill the bottle with water. Your self-watering system is now complete.

What do the small openings on the bottom of the cup do?

Through the openings, air can move in and out. When plants develop roots, they use oxygen. About 20 percent of ordinary air is oxygen.

The capillary action of the water through the wick is the key ingredient in this system. However, you can use any one of the bottle planters to grow a new plant from cuttings.

Growing a New Geranium From an Old Geranium

You can easily reproduce a geranium using your self-watering system. It only takes two or three weeks to grow roots, and it can be grown any time of the year.

For this activity, you need:

○ an adult helper
○ a knife
○ a pop bottle planter filled with a sand and soil mixture
○ an old geranium plant
○ a pencil

From *Showy Science* published by GoodYearBooks. Copyright ©1994 by Hy Kim.

To do this activity:

Look at an old geranium plant. Leaves are alternately arranged, and the growing portions are at the end of each branch. The growing portion is called the *terminal bud*.

Pick off a stem that has a terminal bud as in the illustration. Have an adult make a clean cut about 10 centimeters long directly across the stem with a sharp knife. If the cut is in the middle of the stem, cut it only about 5 to 7 centimeters long. Trim off most of the leaves, leaving only two or three near the terminal bud.

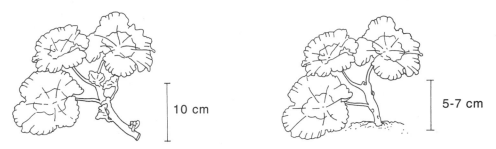

10 cm   5-7 cm

Use a pencil or your finger to make a hole in the sand and soil mixture. Make it long enough to cover the cutting up to its lowest leaf. Press the sand and soil mixture down firmly around the cutting.

Place the system on your windowsill for a few weeks. The cutting will develop roots and grow new leaves. The new plant is on its way to becoming an independent plant. The next experiment explains why it is necessary to trim off some of the leaves first.

A Water Evaporation Contest

Green leaves perspire just as we do. Green leaves release water vapor through little pores called *stomata* which are on the underside of the leaves. These release water vapor to take away excess heat from the leaves. Without this cooling system, many leaves would be cooked in the summer! As a result of plant perspiration, an enormous amount of water evaporates into the air. This activity gives you a chance to observe plant perspiration.

For this activity, you need:

- ○ four pieces of paper towel
- ○ four drinking straws
- ○ two baby food jars
- ○ water

To do this activity:

Make four wicks by rolling each piece of paper towel. Insert one paper towel wick into each drinking straw. Unfold the end of one wick and design two leaves like those shown. Do this for the other three wicks.

Pour an equal amount of water into each baby food jar. Put one straw with two paper towel leaves in one jar. Put three straws with a total of six leaves in the other jar.

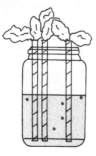

Watch the water levels in the jars for a few days. What happens?

From *Showy Science* published by GoodYearBooks. Copyright ©1994 by Hy Kim.

From which jar does more water evaporate?

The water evaporates more quickly if there are many leaves in the system. The reason why we have to trim the flower buds and all but two or three leaves is to prevent excess water loss through too many leaves. Stem cuttings without roots cannot supply as much water as stems with roots. You have to trim off some small branches and leaves of a plant that you are transplanting for the same reason. Your plant may lose many root hairs when you transplant it.

Growing an African Violet From a Leaf Cutting

For this activity, you need:

- ○ an African violet plant
- ○ a pair of scissors
- ○ a bottle planter filled with sand and soil mixture

To do this activity:

Cut off about 3 centimeters of the leaf stalk (*petiole*) of a healthy African violet leaf. Dry out the sap from the cutting by exposing the leaf to air for a while.

Make a hole in the sand and soil mixture of the bottle planter. Insert the stalk in the hole so the lower part of the leaf touches the sand and soil mixture. Press the sand and soil mixture around the stalk. Add water as needed.

In several months, new leaves will develop near the joint of the stalk and leaf.

new leaves

The bottle planter is very handy for growing a new plant from a cutting because it **does** not require frequent watering. You can also use this method to grow new **gloxinia** plants.

Growing a Peperomia Plant From a Leaf Cutting

For this activity, you need:

- ○ a peperomia plant
- ○ a pair of scissors
- ○ a bottle planter filled with a sand and soil mixture
- ○ a pencil

To do this activity:

Cut a leaf attached to about 7 centimeters of leaf stalk. Dry out the sap. Make a hole in the sand and soil mixture with a pencil. Insert 4 centimeters of the stalk into the hole. Press the sand and soil mixture around the stalk.

In **a** few months, a new stem and leaves will grow from the old stalk.

From *Showy Science* published by GoodYearBooks. Copyright ©1994 by Hy Kim.

new plant

You can grow new plants from stem cuttings for a wandering Jew, coleus, or snake plant. Some climbing roses, currants, grapes, forsythia, lilac, chrysanthemum, pussy willow, and box wood are also known to grow from cuttings.

Wandering Jew
(Tradescantia)

Coleus

Growing a Rex Begonia from a Leaf Cutting

For this activity, you need:

○ a healthy rex begonia leaf

○ several bottle planters filled with a sand and soil mixture

To do this activity:

Select a healthy leaf. Cut it into triangular sections as shown below. Make sure that each section has at least one of the large veins of the leaf. Dry out the sappy cuttings by exposing them to the air for a few hours.

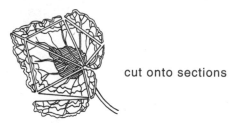

cut onto sections

Plant each section in a bottle planter. A young plant will grow from each cutting.

new plant

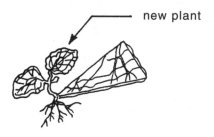

Growing a Spider Plant From an Offset

Each plant has its own ways of reproducing. Some can be grown from offsets, roots, bulbs, or tubers. In order to grow a new spider plant from an offset, you need a spider plant with offsets and a bottle planter filled with a sand and soil mixture. The illustration below shows a spider plant with an offset.

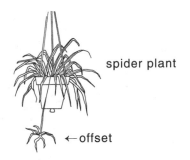

spider plant

← offset

For this activity, you need:

○ a spider plant offset
○ a pop bottle planter or regular planting pot

To do this activity:

Separate the offset from the stem and plant it in a bottle planter or regular planting pot.

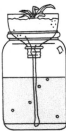

Within several weeks, the offset will grow roots and become an independent spider plant. In a natural setting, offsets grow into independent plants when they touch the ground. This way, spider plants can heavily populate certain areas.

The spider plant is one example of a plant that produces offsets for growing new plants. The hen-and-chicks plant, strawberry, water hyacinth, and water lettuce are some other plants that grow new plants through offsets.

Growing Plants From a Potato and a Sweet Potato

Growing a new plant from either a potato or a sweet potato is fun and easy.

To grow a sweet potato plant, you need:

- ◯ a sweet potato
- ◯ a wide-mouthed jar
- ◯ some rocks
- ◯ water
- ◯ a small lump of charcoal
- ◯ a pencil

To do this activity:

Select a sweet potato with eyes (sprouts) that are clearly visible. (Some sweet potatoes in a grocery store are treated so that they do not sprout. Make sure yours is untreated.) Put some rocks and water in a jar. Place the sweet potato on the rocks. The lower part of the sweet potato should be submerged in water. Add more water as needed.

Add a small lump of charcoal to the water to prevent a bad odor and to keep the sweet potato from rotting. Roots and stems will grow from the sweet potato.

You can grow sweet potato plants in your garden from stem cuttings. As the stems grow longer, cut them to a length of about 10 centimeters. Trim off all the leaves except two or three near the top.

From *Showy Science* published by GoodYearBooks. Copyright ©1994 by Hy Kim.

stem cutting

Dry the stem for a while. Use a pencil to make slanted holes in the garden soil. Insert one stem per hole. Press the soil around the stem. Water your sweet potato plant as often as you water your garden.

in the garden soil

You may root the stem in a bottle planter and then transplant it to your garden. Later, you can harvest sweet potatoes from your garden. Since a sweet potato is a root, you are growing a new plant from a root.

in the bottle planter

To grow a potato plant, you need:

- ◯ a potato
- ◯ a wide-mouthed jar
- ◯ some rocks
- ◯ water
- ◯ a small lump of charcoal
- ◯ a pencil

To do this activity:

You can grow new plants from a potato with the same procedure you used for a sweet potato. Either place a potato on some rocks in a jar or suspend a potato in a bottle with toothpicks as shown in the next illustration.

As the roots grow long, arrange the water level in the jar so that only the roots are submerged in the water. This way, the potato has less chance of rotting.

You can experiment with the sprouting potato. Do the potato's stem and roots grow more quickly in a dark place or a sunny place? How about in a warm place or a cool place?

More information about the potato:

The potato is a tuber. This is a thickened part of a stem which is found beneath the soil. In a tuber, there are many eyes from which new plants can be grown. Potato, Jerusalem artichoke, and begonia-evansiana plants can be grown from tubers.

For a similar activity:

Carrots, turnips, and pineapples are also roots. You can grow these new plants in a jar using the same procedure as you did for a sweet potato.

Find a carrot, turnip, or pineapple with some stems and leaves showing on top. Cut off about five centimeters from the top of the plant. Place your cutting in a jar or a tray with pebbles and water as shown. Roots and stems will then develop.

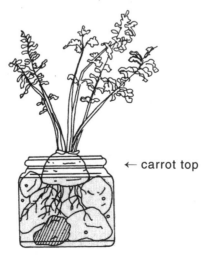

← carrot top

From *Showy Science* published by GoodYearBooks. Copyright ©1994 by Hy Kim.

Does a Sprouting Potato Need Fresh Air?

Does a sprouting potato need fresh air? If so, why? This question can be applied to any sprouting seed or cutting. An experiment will help you find the answer.

For this activity, you need:

- ○ two potatoes
- ○ two jars (one with a cap)
- ○ some rocks
- ○ water

To do this activity:

Place one potato in a jar on the rocks or suspend it in a jar with toothpicks. Add water to the jar until its level touches the potato.

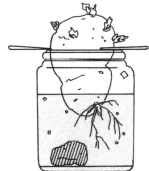

Place the other potato into a jar of water. Tightly screw the cap on the jar. Make a hypothesis as to which one will grow roots and stems first. Explain your hypothesis.

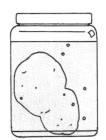

The potato on the rocks will grow roots and stems first. The potato in the air-tight jar may grow some roots and even stems, but it will do so very slowly.

Why does this happen?

The potato in the air-tight jar will eventually rot because it stays in water for a long period of time. A potato has less chance of rotting if it grows roots and stems early. In the process of growing roots and stems, the potato needs oxygen. The potato exposed to air will get its necessary oxygen. The potato in the air-tight jar has only a limited amount of oxygen available to it.

What Is Hydroponics?

Hydroponics is the practice of growing plants without soil. Water, sand, rocks, plant remains, and plant nutrients are used in place of soil. Compared to regular farming, hydroponics has some advantages. It does not require weeding. It requires less labor. It is also very clean, and any plant-growing experiment using hydroponics is more precise and controllable.

Many plant growth activities in this book are hydroponic. For example, the activity of growing a new plant from a sweet potato is hydroponic. The following illustration shows a decorative sweet potato plant.

For this activity, you need:

◯ the sweet potato plant from your earlier experiment
◯ plant food

To do this activity:

As the roots and stems grow from a sweet potato, suspend the sweet potato on the jar so that it does not touch water. You may replace the jar with a milk bottle as in the illustration. Place the system on the windowsill so that the plant can get sunlight but the water can stay in the shade. Add some plant food to the water (follow the directions on the plant food package). The stems will grow to cover a large area.

Growing New Plants From Bulbs

Plants such as narcissus, hyacinth, tulip, and onion store food in their underground bulbs. They die when the winter cold approaches. The fate of the new leaves and flowers for the coming season is already stored in the past year's bulbs.

For this activity, you need:

○ hyacinth, tulip, or narcissus bulbs

○ a container

○ some pebbles

○ water

To do this activity:

Fill a container half-full of small pebbles. Place two or three bulbs on this pebble layer, and place some more pebbles around them to keep the bulbs in place. Pour water into the container until the water level reaches the bottom of the bulbs.

If you do this activity in early winter, set the container in a dark place that is cold (not freezing) for a few weeks. After the bulbs develop roots, bring the container into normal room temperature.

If you do this activity in the middle of spring, the bulbs will grow roots and flower at room temperature. If you cannot find the flowering bulbs, you can grow an onion plant by the same method.

Place a healthy onion on the pebbles. Fill the container with water until the water level reaches to the bottom of the onion. A small lump of charcoal in the water will prevent the onion from rotting. Roots and stems will develop.

ACTIVITIES FOR
EXPLORING
MICROBES

Rotting Banana Slices With Yeast

Microbes are living things that are so small that we cannot see them without the aid of a microscope. However, they do many incredible things around us and for us. Yeast is a one-celled plant that is an easy and safe microbe for study. In this activity, you can demonstrate how quickly yeast will rot away a banana slice.

For this activity, you need:

- ❍ two jars
- ❍ a banana
- ❍ a package of yeast

To do this activity:

Slice the banana in half lengthwise and peel off its skin (either partially or completely). Place one slice in each jar. Sprinkle some yeast on one of the slices. Loosely replace the lids. Place the bottles in a warm place, and check them in a few days. You will see the banana sprinkled with yeast decaying and shrinking more rapidly than the other slice.

What is happening to the banana slice and the yeast?

Yeast eats the banana and breaks it down into different kinds of raw materials. One of these raw materials produced by yeast is carbon dioxide gas. Because yeast breaks down wastes, food, and dead organisms into raw materials, it is called a *decomposer*. Yeast and many other small decomposers help the world run smoothly by recycling raw materials. Why is the other banana slice, which was not sprinkled with yeast, also decaying? Some yeast spores and other microbes that are always present in the air landed on the slice.

From *Showy Science* published by GoodYearBooks. Copyright ©1994 by Hy Kim.

A Bottle of Carbon Dioxide Gas

By growing yeast, you can show that microbes break sugar down into gas and alcohol. You can collect a bottleful of gas and prove that it is carbon dioxide. Then you can use this gas in a number of experiments.

For this activity, you need:

○ a jar
○ a bottle thin enough to fit inside the jar
○ any starchy food or sugar
○ a package of yeast

To do this activity:

Place some sugar or starchy food and some yeast in the bottle. Fill the bottle halfway with warm water. Shake the bottle so that the contents mix, and fill it to the top with warm water.

Cover the filled bottle with the jar as shown.

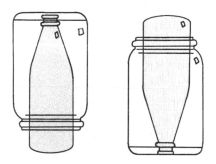

Press the bottle and jar together and flip them over. If the bottle stands on its opening without disturbance, the water will not flow out. Even though it is unnecessary, you may add some water to the jar. Place the system in a warm place. Within a few hours, you may be able to see the gas accumulating on the top of the bottle. The gas will push the water out of the bottle.

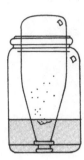

Within a day (depending on the temperature), the bottle will be filled with gas. The sugar or starchy food has changed into other things: one of which is in the gas, and the other is in the water.

Press the bottle and jar together, and drain the liquid into another container. Flip the system over to separate the bottle from the system. Remove the jar and replace the cap on the bottle of gas.

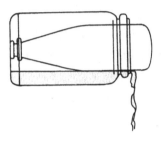

From *Showy Science* published by GoodYearBooks. Copyright ©1994 by Hy Kim.

To explore further...
Do these activities:

For this activity, you need:

○ an adult helper
○ the bottle of gas from the above activity
○ a candle
○ matches

To do this activity:

Whenever you perform an experiment with fire, be sure to do it under the supervision of an adult! As in the illustration, hold the bottle of gas near the flame of a candle.

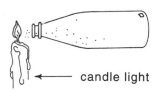

← candle light

As the gas flows out of the bottle, the flame will weaken and die. Carbon dioxide does not support combustion. As the carbon dioxide reaches the candle wick, it pushes away other air in which oxygen gas is mixed. Lack of oxygen makes the flame die.

For this activity, you need:

○ lime water
○ the bottle of gas

To do this activity:

Ask your science teacher for some lime water. You can change the clear lime water into a milky white liquid simply by pouring the lime water into the bottle of gas. In fact, this is the test for carbon dioxide. In the lime water experiment, the dissolved lime (CaO) chemically combines with the carbon dioxide (CO_2) to make small particles of limestone ($CaCO_3$) that look milky. Carbon dioxide is an ingredient in the food-making process of green plants called *photosynthesis*.

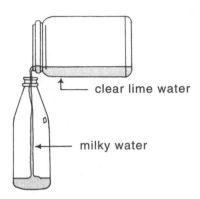

clear lime water

milky water

For this activity, you need:

○ water

○ a slice of bread

○ a jar with a lid, filled with carbon dioxide (use the first activity to help you create this)

To do this activity:

Does mold grow in carbon dioxide? You can conduct an experiment that will help you find the answer to this question. Sprinkle some water droplets on a slice of bread. Place the bread in a jar, loosely replacing its lid. Sprinkle some water droplets on another slice of bread. Place this slice in a carbon dioxide-filled jar. Keep the two jars in a warm, shady place for a few days. Observe what happens.

air

carbon dioxide

As a decomposer, mold needs oxygen to break food down into raw materials. Therefore, mold will grow in the jar filled with air but not in the jar filled with carbon dioxide.

For this activity, you need:

○ a jar with a lid, filled with air

○ a jar with a lid, filled with carbon dioxide (see the above activity to create this)

○ lima beans

○ water

To do this activity:

Another interesting experiment is seeing if sprouting seeds do well in carbon dioxide. To set up the experiment, place some lima beans in two jars, one filled with ordinary air and the other filled with carbon dioxide. Add a few drops of water to each jar. Tighten the lids.

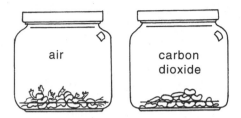

Check on them for the next few days. Can you make a hypothesis about which jar's seeds will sprout first and why? Even though all green plants need carbon dioxide in their food-making process, the seeds in the carbon dioxide-filled jar will not sprout because they need oxygen, too. The sprouting seeds, which use food already made, are not capable of making their own food yet. As they use food, they need oxygen to get energy.

Does Yeast Grow Better in a Warm Place or a Cold Place?

Let's take another look at yeast and find out about where and how it grows best.

For this activity, you need:

- ❍ liquid from your earlier banana-yeast activity
- ❍ 2 microscope slides
- ❍ an eye dropper
- ❍ a microscope or magnifying glass
- ❍ two spoonfuls of sugar
- ❍ four pinches of packaged yeast
- ❍ water
- ❍ two bottles
- ❍ two jars

To do this activity:

If a microscope is available, you may be able to see the tiny yeast plants. First, place one drop of the liquid from your earlier banana-yeast activity on a slide. Cover the slide with another slide, and place them on the stage of the microscope. Focus with the low-power and high-power lenses. You may be able to see the yeast, which is a one-celled fungus.

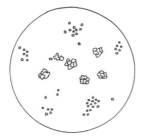

Yeast is an incredible organism. It lives almost everywhere on earth. If it meets unfavorable conditions, such as lack of food, extreme hot or cold temperatures, or lack of moisture, some of the yeast cells change into spores and wait until favorable

From *Showy Science* published by GoodYearBooks. Copyright ©1994 by Hy Kim.

conditions return. If the favorable conditions return or if the spores land on a place that meets these conditions, they eat the food and multiply in large numbers. In nature, yeast spores move by wind, water, and animals.

Now that you know a little about yeast, let's find out what conditions are best for yeast to grow. First, mix one spoonful of sugar, two pinches of yeast, and water in a bottle. Invert the bottle in a jar.

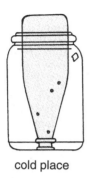
cold place

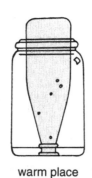
warm place

Make another identical system. Place one in a cold place like a refrigerator and one in a warm place. Observe the two systems the next day.

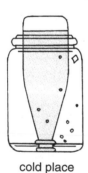
cold place

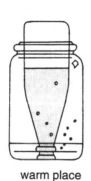
warm place

Where does yeast grow best?

You will find that yeast does not grow as well in the cold place as in the warm place. Temperature is one of the most important growing conditions for yeast and other microbes. The yeast is not dead but waiting for favorable conditions in order to multiply. You can confirm this by moving your bottle from the cold place to the warm place and examining it after a day.

Does Yeast Grow Without Food?

Now you know that yeast needs warmth. Does it also need food to grow? To find out, do this activity.

For this activity, you need:

○ two spoonfuls of sugar

○ four pinches of packaged yeast

○ water

○ two bottles

○ two jars

To do this activity:

First make two systems, as shown in the illustration.

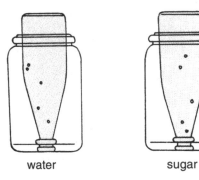

water   sugar

Place water and yeast in one bottle. In the other, combine water, sugar, and yeast. Place the two systems in a warm place and observe what happens.

What does yeast need to grow?

You will see that yeast does not grow in the bottle with plain water, lacking sugar for food. The availability of food is another important growing condition for yeast and other microbes.

From *Showy Science* published by GoodYearBooks. Copyright ©1994 by Hy Kim.

Does Yeast Grow Better in a Dry Place or a Moist Place?

Does yeast grow more quickly in a dry place or a wet place? This activity will help you find the answer.

For this activity, you need:

- ○ two spoonfuls of sugar
- ○ four pinches of packaged yeast
- ○ water
- ○ two bottles
- ○ two jars

To do this activity:

Place sugar and yeast in one bottle. In another bottle, mix sugar, water, and yeast as in the illustration. Wait one day and observe what happens.

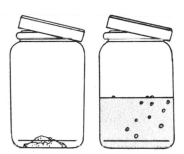

Does yeast need water to grow?

You will find that nothing has happened in the bottle without water. However, you will also find that the yeast has multiplied many times in the bottle with water. Water is very important for yeast and other microbes to grow.

Does Yeast Grow Better in a Sunny Place or a Shady Place?

Does yeast grow more quickly in a sunny place or a shady place? To find out the answer, do this activity.

For this activity, you need:

- ○ two spoonfuls of sugar
- ○ four pinches of packaged yeast
- ○ water
- ○ two bottles
- ○ two jars

To do this activity:

Place one system in a sunny place such as a windowsill, and place the other system in a shady place that has the same temperature. Wait one day and observe.

 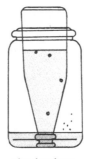

sunny place   shady place

Does yeast need light to grow?

If all other conditions are equal, yeast grows better in a shady place because the ultra-violet light (that's the kind of light that tans your skin) in the sunny place kills some of the yeast. Ultraviolet light is one of the conditions that kills or hinders the growth of yeast and other microbes.

From *Showy Science* published by GoodYearBooks. Copyright ©1994 by Hy Kim.

From Sugar to Alcohol

¡S!

CAUTION: This experiment produces a small quantity of alcohol. Do not drink this or any other liquid that results from an activity or experiment.

As yeast grows, it breaks down sugar into carbon dioxide and alcohol. This process is called *fermentation*. We call this process *anaerobic*, because it does not use any air. You can make alcohol in your home or at school.

For this activity, you need:

○ a one-gallon apple juice bottle, filled halfway with a mixture of:
   warm water, a cup of sugar, and a package of yeast
○ an adult helper
○ a smaller jar with a cap
○ tubing
○ an index card
○ a flat container or pan filled halfway with water

To do this activity:

Fill the bottle halfway with the mixture of warm water, sugar, and yeast. Mix and replace the cap loosely. Place the bottle in a warm place for a few days.

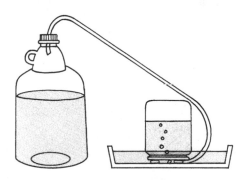

To collect carbon dioxide, attach a collecting system as shown. Have an adult drill a hole in the cap. Insert one end of some tubing in the hole and seal the joint with rubber cement. Put the other end of the tubing in a container of water. Fill a bottle

to the top with water, which will collect the gas. Place an index card over the mouth of the bottle and flip the bottle. Put the mouth of the bottle into the water in the large container. Remove the index card and place one end of the tubing inside the mouth of the bottle as shown in the illustration.

You may support the gas-collecting bottle in the container by adding clay or rocks between the rim of the bottle and the bottom of the container. The carbon dioxide bubbles will rise to the top of the gas-collecting bottle, pushing out water into the water container. In this way, you can collect large amounts of carbon dioxide.

How can you tell that there is alcohol in the liquid?

You may be able to detect a strange alcohol smell from the liquid.

You can separate the alcohol from the water by using a system similar to the one shown in the following illustration. To do this, you need an adult's supervision.

For this activity, you need:

○ an adult helper
○ a one-gallon apple cider bottle with a cap
○ tubing
○ a large pot, such as a stockpot
○ a hot plate
○ water
○ a smaller bottle
○ a container into which the smaller bottle will fit
○ cold water

To do this activity:

Arrange the system as in the illustration. A tall pot is better than a short one. The alcohol-collecting bottle should be submerged in cold water. Place a few rocks or spoons between the pot and the bottle so that the bottom of the bottle does not touch the pot. Slowly warm the water in the pot by turning on a hot plate or stove upon which the pot is placed.

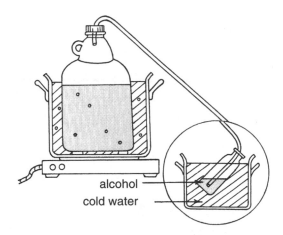

alcohol
cold water

What happens to the alcohol?

As the liquid inside the bottle reaches 80° Celsius (173°F), the alcohol in the small bottle will start to boil and change into gas, thereby expanding its volume and pushing through the tubing. The gas will condense into liquid again in the cold alcohol-collecting bottle.

Water or alcohol in the liquid phase will change to the gas phase as it is heated. The gaseous water and alcohol will condense into liquid again as they are cooled. Alcohol boils at 78.4°C, but water boils at 100°C. If you maintain the temperature of the liquid in the bottle at 70-80°C, you can collect highly concentrated alcohol. If you boil the liquid at a higher temperature than 80°C, more water will be in the distilled liquid.

When you dismantle the distillation system, remove the tubing from the alcohol bottle before turning off the hot plate or stove. Otherwise, the alcohol will be drawn into the yeast bottle because the air in the bottle contracts as it cools.

For a related activity, you need:

○ an adult helper

○ a piece of paper

○ an old dish

○ a match

○ the bottle of alcohol from the previous activity

To do this activity:

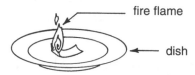

fire flame

dish

As shown, you may do a flame test under an adult's supervision. Dip a small piece of paper into the alcohol. Put the paper on a dish, and light it with a match. The resulting flame proves that it is alcohol.

More information about fermentation:

When the yeast decomposes sugar into alcohol (called *grain alcohol* or *ethanol*) and carbon dioxide, it gains energy that is released by the decomposition process. Yeast uses the energy to reproduce. About 32 grams of simple sugar (1 mole) have 673 kilocalories. This simple sugar has been made by green plants through photosynthesis. In the process of photosynthesis, 673 kilocalories of solar energy is used to combine carbon dioxide and water into sugar. As the yeast decomposes one mole of sugar molecules into carbon dioxide and alcohol, it uses 20 kilocalories of energy and stores 653 kilocalories of energy in the alcohol. When we burn the alcohol, we release the energy stored in it.

If we use up all the fossil fuels like gasoline in the future, we may be able to rely partly on alcohol fermented from grains and garbage by yeast. Gasoline is not a renewable fuel but alcohol is.

Growing Bread Molds

You probably have seen mold on bread or on rotten fruits. However, you may not have paid attention to it. By growing bread mold, you can learn many things about mold and microbes.

For this activity, you need:

- ◯ two slices of bread
- ◯ two peanut butter jars
- ◯ water
- ◯ a piece of cloth
- ◯ a rubber band

To do this activity:

Sprinkle several drops of water on each slice of bread. Wipe the bread on a smooth surface of the floor so that you collect some dust particles on the slices. Place a slice of bread in a jar and screw on the lid.

Place the second slice of bread in the other jar. Cover its mouth with a piece of cloth and secure it with a rubber band.

Place the two jars side by side in a warm, shady place. You may loosen the cap on the closed jar so that some fresh air can get inside. Observe the slices of bread for several days to a week.

Predict in which jar more mold will grow and why. You may have results like this:

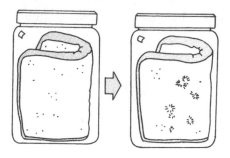

One or two spots of mold may appear on the slice of bread in the air-tight jar. On the other hand, many mold colonies may appear on the slice of bread in the jar covered with only a cloth.

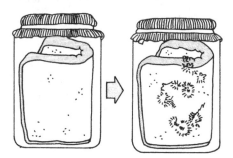

Even though bread molds are plants, they do not have chlorophyll. Most green plants use chlorophyll to make food during photosynthesis. Without chlorophyll, mold uses food made by others. Like most animals, mold needs oxygen to use the food. A limited amount of oxygen in the covered jar allows some mold to grow. In the loosely covered jar, plenty of oxygen is exchanged, allowing rapid mold growth. You may see different kinds of mold on the slice of bread.

How did the mold get on the slice of bread?

Microscopic mold spores are almost everywhere around us: in the air, soil, and water. When you wiped the smooth surface of the floor with the moist bread at the beginning of this experiment, many mold spores were picked up by the bread.

Looking Into Bread Molds

Now it's time to take a much closer look at mold!

For this activity, you need:

- ○ a magnifying glass or microscope
- ○ a glass microscope slide
- ○ a slide cover
- ○ a toothpick
- ○ water

To do this activity:

To observe mold, take the moldy slice of bread out of the jar and look at the mold colonies through a magnifying glass. If you have a microscope, place a bit of the mold on the glass slide and place the cover over the mold. Look at the mold through a high-power lens.

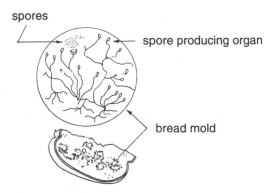

spores

spore producing organ

bread mold

The bread mold (*rhizopus*) looks like small black dots connected with silky white threads, as shown in the illustration above. The white threads spread around and develop the small dots. The dots are spore-producing organs. As the organs mature, thousands of tiny spores from each dot are spread around by the movement of the air.

Dip one end of a toothpick in water and rub the wet end on a slide to make a wet spot. Touch the black dots with the wet end of the toothpick, and then rub the end on the wet spot of the slide. Place a cover slide on the wet spot. Look at the spot through the low-power objective and then the high-power objective. You will see many spore cells. Each black dot releases about fifty thousand spores in the air, much like a dandelion spreads its seeds in the wind. Each spore will sprout and develop a mold colony if it lands on food and the other growing conditions are met.

Common mold (*mucor*) grows on bread, too. It looks like spots of different colors. If you look at them through a magnifying glass or microscope, the colonies look like the veins of a leaf, as shown below. You may be able to find blue-green molds, black molds, gray molds, or even pink molds on the bread.

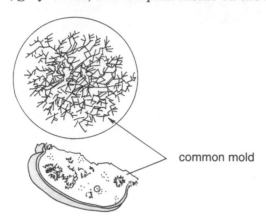

common mold

Spore-producing organs develop in the colonies, and the spores spread in the wind like the bread mold.

How does mold digest food?

If mold is growing on food, the mold digests the food differently from the way we digest our food. The digestive fluids spread out in the food and break it down into simple nutrients. Then the simple nutrients pass through the cell membranes of the mold. Almost all microbes digest their food in much the same way. The molds break down dead organisms into raw materials which plants can use in their food-making process.

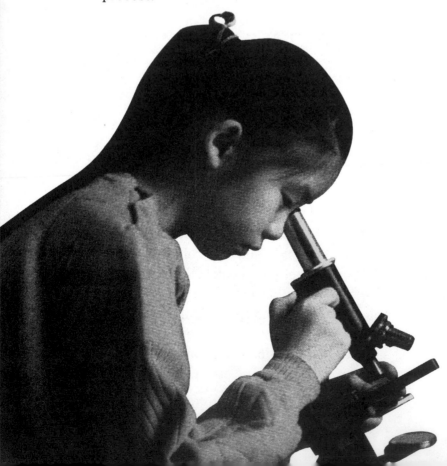

Growing Bread Mold From Spores

Microscopic cells called *spores* are the seeds of mold. If a spore lands on moist food such as bread, the shell of the spore dissolves, and a new bread mold grows by cell division. Tiny root-like threads, called *hyphae*, grow downward into the food and bring nutrients. Tiny threads grow over the surface of the food and produce stalks that rise above the bread. On the top of each stalk is a ball that is the spore-producing organ. As the organs mature, millions of spores scatter about in moving air. In this activity, you will use mold spores that you have grown to develop mold colonies.

For this activity, you need:

○ the mold you grew in an earlier activity
○ a slice of bread
○ water
○ a toothpick

To do this activity:

Sprinkle a few drops of water on a slice of bread. Wet one end of a toothpick. Rub the wet end of the toothpick on the mold that was grown in the previous experiment. Wipe the spores on a spot on the new slice of bread so that mold spores remain on the spot.

Place the slice of bread in a jar. Cover the mouth of the jar with a piece of cloth as in the next illustration. Place the jar in a warm, shady place. Watch what happens. Soon you will see a mold colony developing on the spot where you placed the mold spores.

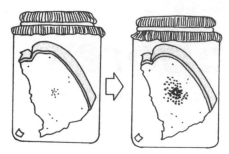

More information about mold:

Like many other microbes, mold spores exist almost everywhere around us. If they land on a spot where they meet favorable conditions (food, temperature, moisture), they grow, produce more spores, and die.

Growing Blue-Green Molds

Blue-green molds became well known after Professor Alexander Fleming of London discovered a wonder drug called *penicillin* in 1928. He was studying a microbe that causes boils and other infections in human beings. In one of his microbe cultures, a blue-green mold colony accidentally grew. To his amazement, the microbe that causes boils was killed by the blue-green mold.

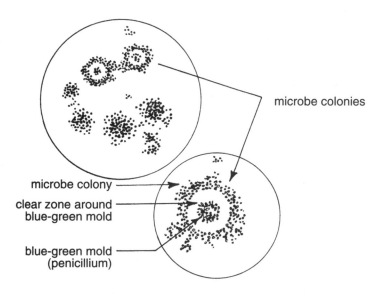

microbe colonies

microbe colony

clear zone around
blue-green mold

blue-green mold
(penicillium)

A product of the blue-green mold destroyed the microbes. Professor Fleming named the product that kills the microbes penicillin. He also discovered that penicillin kills many common bacteria. His discovery led to the widespread manufacture of this wonder drug. By growing certain kinds of microbes, we can control the population of other kinds of microbes.

If you grew the bread mold described earlier, you may have grown blue-green molds on the slice of bread. You may grow blue-green molds either by collecting the spores from dust in the air around you or by transferring the spores from blue-green molds that you find.

For this activity, you need:

○ an adult helper
○ moldy bread, oranges, lemons, or bleu cheese
○ a knife
○ a toothpick

To do this activity:

Hunt for blue-green molds around your house. They may be on the surface of moldy bread, oranges, lemons, or bleu cheese. Cut an orange or a lemon in half. With a toothpick, touch some mold and wipe the spores on the freshly cut surface of the orange or lemon.

Place the lemon or orange slice in a jar and loosely replace the lid. Make sure that fresh air can get into the jar.

Place the jar in a warm, shady place. Observe it for a few days. You will see a blue-green mold colony developing on the spot in which you placed the spores. If you magnify it, this blue-green mold looks like the following illustration.

The threads are silky and white. From the threads, many upright threads develop. At the end of the upright thread, many tiny branches develop. These tiny branches develop strings of blue-green spores. One branch of an upright thread with spores looks like a brush. The Latin word for brush is *penicillium*; thus, blue-green mold is called penicillium. The total colony of penicillium looks green because of numerous green spores.

If you cannot find blue-green molds around your house and want to grow them, wipe the dust from a smooth surface on furniture or a windowsill with the cut side of a lemon or orange. Place the half-piece of fruit in a jar, as in the previous experiment. You will see blue-green mold in a few days.

How Quickly Do Bacteria Grow?

If bacteria, a type of microbe, has ideal growing conditions—moisture, temperature, food—it splits into two microbes every twenty minutes. Forty minutes later, the two microbes divide into four. When a microbe grows to a certain predetermined size, it divides itself into two microbes instead of growing into a bigger animal with many cells. How many microbes do you think will appear one or two days later under favorable conditions? To answer this question, do some calculations.

For this activity, you need:

○ a calculator

To do this activity:

Can you fill in the ?s in the chart by calculating the numbers? For example, one day later, the number of bacteria will be 2^{72}, which means that you must continue multiplying 2 by 2 by 2 until you have multiplied 72 2s, or 4,722,366,483,000,000,000,000! This is an incredibly large number of bacteria! However, many variables, such as scarce

From *Showy Science* published by GoodYearBooks. Copyright ©1994 by Hy Kim.

food supply or buildup of body wastes, come into play and alter the bacterial growth rate. Usually bacterial growth passes through a rapid growing stage, a plateau stage in which the growth and death rates are the same, and a declining stage.

Bacterial Fision Every 20 Minutes

Time	Cal	No. Bacteria
0:00	2^0	2/2=1
0:20	2^1	2x1=2
0:40	2^2	2x2=4
1:00	2^3	2x2x2=8
1:20	2^4	2x2x2x2=16
1:40	2^5	2x2x2x2x2=32
2:00	2^6	2x2x2x2x2x2=64
2:20	2^7	2x2x2x2x2x2x2=128
24:00	2^{72}	?s
48:00	2^{144}	?s

More information about bacteria:

Even though many different kinds of bacteria exist, they are usually divided into three groups by their general appearance: spherical shape (*cocci*), cylindrical shape (*bacilli*), and spiral rod shape (*spirilla*).

Bacteria that have the ability to form spores can live through extreme conditions of cold, heat, dryness, and lack of food. (Mold spores are reproductive, while bacterial spores are a survival means.) If the spores meet favorable conditions, they multiply very quickly.

The Germ Theory of Disease and Our Defense Systems

Nineteenth-century scientists were the first to believe and prove that diseases are caused by microbes. Before that time, not only did people not know the cause of disease, but they also couldn't cure the diseases appropriately. Superstitions, witches, and rituals were commonly used to treat many diseases. Now we know that microbes are the cause of many diseases, and they are everywhere: in the air, water, and soil.

Fortunately, our bodies are well prepared for an invasion of microbes. Covering the outer surface of our body, the skin is our first line of defense from invading microbes.

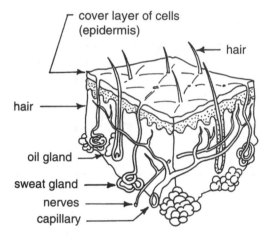

cover layer of cells (epidermis)

hair

hair

oil gland

sweat gland

nerves

capillary

The outer layer of skin cells is compact and tough. As cells divide at the bottom of the outer layer, the old cells push outward, flatten, compact, and die. Gradually the dead cells wear out. When you take a bath, the "white dirt" coming from your skin is dead cells. When the dead skin layer is wet, it is good food for some microbes. Sweat has some chemicals that kill microbes. However, when sweat combines with dirty particles and dead cells, microbes may find all the favorable conditions: moisture, food, warmth, and shade.

Small colonies of microbes can develop in the pores of sweat glands or oil glands. This is one reason why you should take a shower after vigorous exercise. Athlete's foot is a disease caused by fungi usually found between the toes. The fungi may find all of the favorable conditions between wet toes. Ringworm is another fungi skin disease common in humans.

From *Showy Science* published by GoodYearBooks. Copyright ©1994 by Hy Kim.

Our teeth can be victims of microbes if we neglect to take care of them. If food remains between teeth, some microbes will find all the favorable conditions in your mouth: food, moisture, warmth, and shelter from ultraviolet light. Microbes produce waste acids that work tirelessly to make a cavity in your teeth.

Microbes that come into our stomach are killed by strong hydraulic acid in the stomach. In addition, our respiratory system has a marvelous defense system from microbes' invasion.

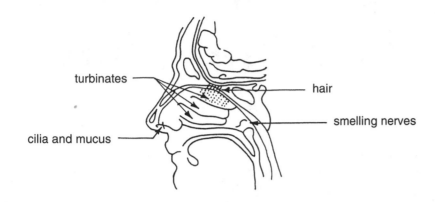

If you look into your nostrils with a mirror, you may see many hairs standing up along the edges. These hairs act as air filters when you inhale. Microscopic hairs called *cilia* and sticky liquid called *mucus* cover the interior of your nasal cavity so any microbes that pass the filtering system can be trapped in the mucus. Cilia moves in wavelike motion so that trapped microbes and dust particles are pushed out of the system. *Turbinates* are structures that make the inhaled air move around the nasal cavity to warm, moisten, and purify the air by mucus before it goes to the lungs.

A certain amount of moisture in the air, particularly in the winter, will help to maintain the moisture level of the mucus in your respiratory system. Some people catch colds and get sore throats easily in dry air because the lack of moisture in the air dries up the mucus. Therefore, more microbes in the inhaled air reach further into the respiratory system.

If microbes invade our body system through a cut in the skin, white blood cells will approach and swallow them. Our body has a remarkable defense system against microbes.

How Does the Salting of Food Prevent Microbes From Spoiling Food?

¡S!

In order to preserve food for long periods of time, we use many different methods, such as boiling, canning, freezing, smoking, pickling, drying, sugaring, exposing it to ultraviolet light, and salting. All of these methods are used to kill microbes and to prevent microbes from growing in the food. Salting certain foods is an efficient method to prevent microbes from growing in the food. The following simple experiment will help you understand why salting is a method to preserve food.

For this activity, you need:

- ○ an adult helper
- ○ a carrot
- ○ two drinking glasses
- ○ a knife

To do this activity:

Fill the glasses halfway with water. Stir salt into the water of one glass. Keep adding more salt until no more can be dissolved. Place one carrot piece in the glass with plain water, and place the other piece of carrot in the salt water.

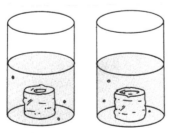

After a few hours, compare the sizes of the carrot pieces.

From *Showy Science* published by GoodYearBooks. Copyright ©1994 by Hy Kim.

The piece of carrot in the salt water will be smaller, and the piece of carrot in the plain water will be fresh and the same in size.

Why did the salted carrot shrink, and what does that have to do with microbes?

The carrot is made of many cells. Each cell has cell liquid called *cytoplasm*. The cytoplasm contains water and other cell materials. When the water concentration of the cytoplasm is less than that of the water outside of the cell, the outside water goes through the cell membrane, swelling the cell. This process is called *osmosis*.

When the water concentration of the outside liquid is less than that of the cytoplasm, water in the cytoplasm moves out through the membrane. This process is called *plysmolysis*. As a result of plysmolysis in the carrot cells, the piece of carrot shrunk.

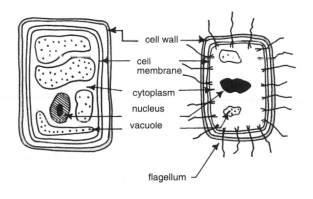

Carrot cell   Bacterial cell

As in the illustration, a bacterial cell is similar to the carrot cell. Plysmolysis will occur in the microbes when they are placed in a liquid like salt water. The microbes cannot survive in those solutions. When the microbes contact solid salt, plysmolysis occurs. Salted fish or pork can last a long time for this reason. Sometimes sugar, which works on the same principle as salt, is used to preserve certain foods.

Microbes in the Community

Microbes spoil food and cause disease in plants, animals, and people. However, what would happen to the world if we didn't have microbes? Dead leaves, plants and animals, and animal body wastes would not decay. Nitrates and other minerals such as calcium and phosphorus would not be freed from dead organisms. Plants would eventually become extinct due to the lack of nitrates and minerals. Dead bodies and body wastes would pile up on the earth if we didn't have microbes. Microbes and other decomposers break down dead organisms and wastes into smaller bits in the soil called humus. The humus makes soil rich and plants can grow and become healthy by recycling necessary minerals.

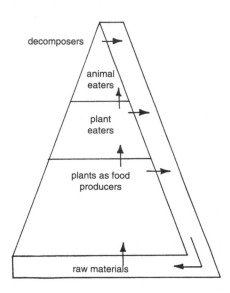

This diagram is a community chart or food pyramid. Plants use raw materials freed by decomposers like microbes from dead organisms and body wastes. Plants are food producers. The plant eaters are the first level of consumers. Insects, deer, rabbits, and most birds are first level consumers. Sometimes first level consumers are called *herbivores*. The eaters of the first level consumers are called second level consumers, or *carnivores*. Foxes, snakes, owls, and bass are second level consumers. Some animals, such as pigs, that eat plants and animals are called *omnivores*. All living things consume food, and the components of the food become part of their bodies. When they die, microbes and other decomposers free the raw materials back into nature. The plants feed on raw materials, and the cycle continues, maintaining life on earth.

From *Showy Science* published by GoodYearBooks. Copyright ©1994 by Hy Kim.

ACTIVITIES FOR
EXPLORING

GRAVITY, MOTION, AND OTHER FORCES

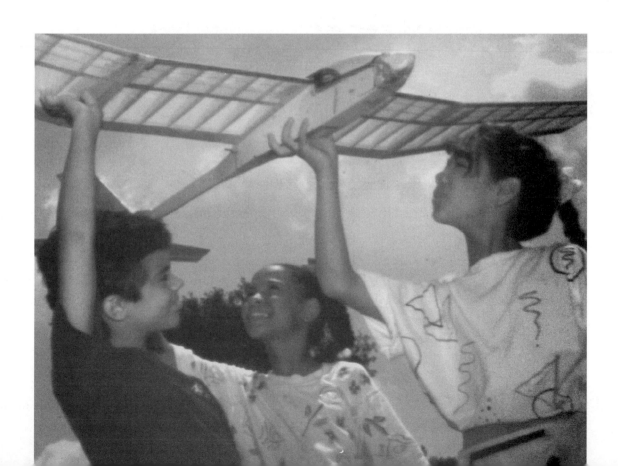

Guess Which One Falls First!

Two identical pieces of aluminum foil are dropped from the same height. Will they strike the floor at the same time? One of the foil pieces is crumpled into a small ball. The ball and the uncrumpled foil piece are dropped from the same height. Which one will strike the floor first? Why?

This is a good activity to demonstrate the concept of the effect of gravity and air resistance on any moving object. This demonstration is especially effective in a small group or class.

For this activity, you need:

○ aluminum foil

○ a pair of scissors

To do this activity:

Fold the aluminum foil and cut out a circle or rectangle. When you unfold the foil, you will have two identically shaped pieces. Hold the foil pieces at the same height. Predict which one will strike the floor first. Drop them and see if your prediction is correct.

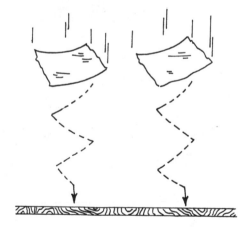

One piece may land a little earlier or later than the other. However, if you try several times, the pieces will often land at the same time.

Now, crumple one of the foil pieces into a small ball. Hold the ball and the other piece of foil at the same height. Drop them at the same time. Predict which one will strike the floor first. The ball will strike the floor first even though both pieces contain the same amount of foil.

From *Showy Science* published by GoodYearBooks. Copyright ©1994 by Hy Kim.

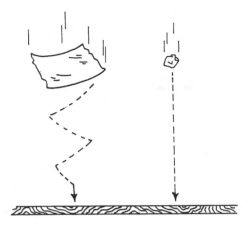

Why does this happen?

The foil pieces fall to the ground because the earth pulls down the objects. This pulling force is called *gravity*. Gravity pulls you and everything around you toward the center of the earth. Even the invisible air around us is pulled toward the earth.

When you drop the foil pieces, they pass through the air to reach the ground. Uncrumpled foil meets more air resistance as it falls than the crumpled foil does. If there was no air resistance, the ball and the piece of foil would reach the ground at the same time. Scientists experimented to prove that idea many years ago. They dropped a feather and an iron ball in a vacuum. The two objects reached the bottom at the same time.

Which Ball Will Strike the Floor First?

Two clay balls, one much bigger than the other, are dropped from the same height. Which ball do you think will strike the floor first? Why?

This simple experiment may cause disagreements among friends. Some will predict that the bigger ball strikes the floor first, and others will guess that they strike the floor at the same time.

For this activity, you need:

- ○ a lump of clay
- ○ a table
- ○ a friend

To do this activity:

To do this activity, you need a lump of clay or Play-Doh©. Make a small ball and a large ball. Have one person climb onto a table top and hold the two balls at the same height. Have the person drop them at the same time. Everyone else should watch the floor to see which one strikes first.

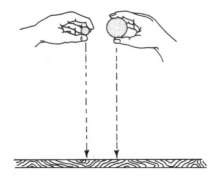

A piece of wood is also a convenient device to help you drop the balls from the same height at the same time. Place the balls on the panel. Hold the panel in the air and flip it over.

Which ball strikes the floor first?

They reach the floor at the same time! The bigger ball meets more air resistance, but it has more mass than the small ball.

Finding the Center of Gravity of a Piece of Cardboard

For this activity, you need:

- ○ cardboard
- ○ scissors
- ○ a string
- ○ a pin
- ○ a pencil
- ○ a large paper clip

To do this activity:

Cut out an irregular shape of cardboard. Balance it on the flat eraser part of a pencil as shown.

Flip over the cardboard and mark the point where you could balance the board on the pencil. This point is the center of gravity. Can you find the center of gravity without the pencil? Some people can guess it accurately and others cannot. Is there any scientific way to find the center of gravity? Yes, there is.

Cut any shape out of a piece of cardboard. Place it on a wall and pin it on a corner. Let the cardboard hang loosely. Tie a paper clip to a string. Hang the string from the pin. Draw a line with a pencil along the string as shown.

Take out the pin and rotate the cardboard. Rotate the cardboard about 90° and pin and mark it.

Draw more lines using the same procedure.

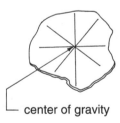

center of gravity

Surprisingly, the lines intersect at one point. This is the center of gravity for the piece of cardboard. You can then balance the piece on a pencil by placing the center of gravity on the point of the eraser.

More information about a center of gravity:

Every object has a center of gravity. This center of gravity is related to the stability of the object on its base. This relationship will be demonstrated in the following three activities.

From *Showy Science* published by GoodYearBooks. Copyright ©1994 by Hy Kim.

Balancing on a Pencil Point

For this activity, you need:

- ○ a spoon
- ○ a fork
- ○ a pencil
- ○ a friend

To do this activity:

Give your friend a spoon, a fork, and a pencil. Ask him or her to balance the fork and spoon on the tip of a pencil lead. Anyone who knows how can do so very simply, but to someone who doesn't know how, it seems impossible.

This task is simple. Join the fork and spoon by sliding the spoon into the tines of the fork. Place them on the tip of the pencil lead as in the illustration. You can carry the fork and spoon by holding the pencil.

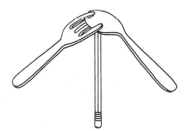

Why does it work?

Every object has a center of gravity. The center of gravity for the spoon and fork is below the base of support, which is the point where the pencil lead touches the spoon. In order to balance an object, its center of gravity should be lower than the base of support. Generally, stability is greater if your support is broader. But in this case, because the center of gravity is lower than the base of support, the spoon and fork are balanced and stable, even though the base of support is just one point.

Balancing a Ruler

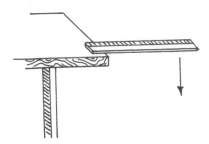

Look at the illustration. If you place one end of a ruler on the edge of a table, the ruler will fall. The task is to keep the ruler balanced as shown without doing anything to the table top. The task seems impossible, doesn't it?

For this activity, you need:

○ a table
○ a ruler
○ string
○ a hammer

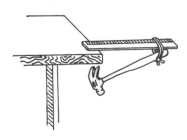

To do this activity:

Using a piece of string tie the ruler to the handle of a hammer. Slide the string and hammer so that the center of gravity is just under the point where the ruler joins the table. The system will balance. If you slide the string and hammer on the ruler to the left, the right end of the ruler will tilt upward. If the center of gravity moves to the right, the ruler will fall.

From *Showy Science* published by GoodYearBooks. Copyright ©1994 by Hy Kim.

Standing an Apple on a Toothpick

For this activity, you need:

- ○ a toothpick
- ○ two apples or potatoes
- ○ a coat hanger

To do this activity:

Poke a toothpick into an apple (or you may substitute a potato). Try to balance the apple on the toothpick as shown. Can you balance the apple on the toothpick without doing anything to the table?

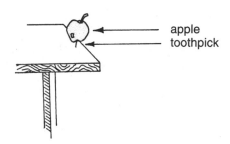

To balance the apple on the toothpick, you need coat hanger wire and another large apple or potato.

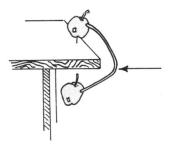

Cut a coat hanger wire to a length of 30-40 centimeters. Bend it in the middle as in the illustration. Poke one end of the wire into the side of the apple. Poke the other end into a large apple under the table. If the center of gravity of the apples and the wire is just below the toothpick, the system will balance. If you tilt the apple on the table, it will return to its original position.

A Pendulum

A great Greek philosopher named Aristotle once made a statement, "To make an object move, you have to apply a force. Once the force stopped acting, the object would stop moving." Sounds true, doesn't it? However, by playing with a pendulum that swung back and forth for a long period of time, Galileo challenged and changed Aristotle's theory.

For this activity, you need:

- ○ two paper clips
- ○ string
- ○ a stick or ruler
- ○ a table
- ○ some weights
- ○ a few metal washers

To do this activity:

Bend a paper clip into an S-shaped hook. Tie a string to the hook. Tie the other end of the string to a stick as shown. Place the stick on a corner of a table. Secure the stick by placing some weights on one end of it. Place a metal washer on the hook. Pull up the washer and let it go. Watch what happens. The washer will swing back and forth.

Why does it keep moving back and forth?

When you first pulled the washer, it moved up in height. When you let it go, the gravity of earth pulled down on the washer. When it reached the bottom of the arc, its kinetic energy carried it up the other side. When the washer stopped on the other side, the gravity pulled the washer back down. This process repeats until air resistance bleeds off all of the energy.

For a similar activity:

Make another pendulum hook of equal length. Place three washers on one hook and one washer on the other hook. Do you think one pendulum will move faster than the other?

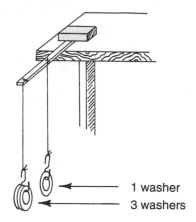

1 washer
3 washers

Pull both pendulums at the same time to the same height, and let them go. Watch their motion. Was your prediction correct?

How does this work?

The two pendulums swing back and forth at equal speed and distance. One complete back-and-forth swing is called a *period*. The number of washers on a pendulum does not affect the period. To vary the period, you may want to make pendulum systems with different lengths of string.

However, the pendulum will eventually stop. Galileo wondered why this happened. To find and answer he performed the following activities.

An Aerodynamic Pendulum

Is an aerodynamic pendulum's swinging motion different than that of a non-aerodynamic pendulum? To find out the answer, you can do a simple experiment.

For this activity, you need:

○ four metal washers
○ two pendulum systems
○ two paper clips

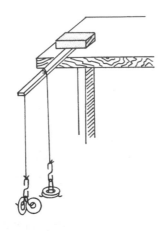

To do this activity:

On one system, connect two washers with a stretched paper clip so that one washer is perpendicular to the other as in the illustration. On the other system, arrange two washers parallel to the floor so that they have less air resistance. This is the aerodynamic pendulum. Pull back the two systems at the same time from the same distance. Let them go, and watch the motions. If you cast shadows of the two pendulums by shining a light from the top of the systems, you can measure the distances that the two pendulums travel.

Which pendulum travels a longer path one minute after the initial push? The aerodynamic pendulum does. This proves that air resistance to the pendulum is one of the reasons why the pendulum eventually stops.

From *Showy Science* published by GoodYearBooks. Copyright ©1994 by Hy Kim.

Showy Science

An Aerodynamic Pendulum String

Does an aerodynamic string of a pendulum make a difference in the swinging motion? To find out the answer, you can do a simple experiment.

For this activity, you need:

○ a strip of tape
○ two pendulum systems

To do this activity:

Tape a strip of masking tape along the string of a pendulum with two washers. Place two washers on the other untaped pendulum system. Pull back the two pendulums at the same time from the same distance. See which one travels a shorter path one minute later. Why does the pendulum with tape on its string slow down first? Air resistance on the string is another reason why the pendulum eventually stops.

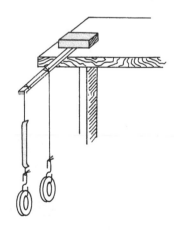

More information about pendulums:

If you swing the pendulum over and over again, the string will eventually break off because of repeated flexing at one spot. When the great scientist Galileo discovered that some of the forces against the swinging pendulum stop its motion, he challenged Aristotle's theory that "to make an object move, you have to apply a force. Once the force stopped acting, the object would stop moving." Galileo believed that if no other forces hindered the pendulum, it would swing forever.

Activities for Exploring Gravity, Motion, and Other Forces

How Does the Foucault Pendulum Work?

Did you ever see a big pendulum tell time by knocking out hour-blocks? This type of pendulum is called a Foucault pendulum. How does it work? A simple demonstration will show you.

For this activity, you need:

○ a metal washer
○ a paper clip
○ string
○ a ruler or pencil
○ a large jar
○ tape
○ a marker

To do this activity:

Using a washer, paper clip, and string, set up a pendulum system as in the illustration. Tape the pencil to the rim of the jar so that it will not move as the pendulum swings. Write E for east, W for west, S for south, and N for north on the jar with a marker.

Start swinging the pendulum east to west. While the pendulum is swinging, slowly turn the jar counterclockwise and watch how the pendulum swings. The pendulum's path will not change as the jar turns. The pendulum will keep swinging in the same direction as the jar is rotated.

Why does this happen?

The earth rotates on its axis, making day and night. Wherever a Foucault pendulum is located, the earth rotates completely in 24 hours but the pendulum traces the same path. If there are 24 blocks around the pendulum and the pendulum swings for 24 hours, it will knock out blocks one by one for 24 hours as the earth rotates beneath the pendulum.

From *Showy Science* published by GoodYearBooks. Copyright ©1994 by Hy Kim.

A Marble Game

By rolling marbles, the participants in this activity apply the scientific concepts of gravity, friction, and inertia.

For this activity, you need:

○ a marble

○ a ramp on which you can roll a marble (You can make a ramp with a manila folder.)

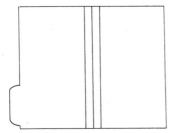

To do this activity:

Open the folder to expose the center fold. Make two creases about 1.5 to 2 centimeters from the center fold.

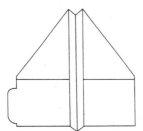

Fold the creases in a "v" shape as in the illustration below. Fold down two upper corners along the creases.

Overlap the folded corners and staple the overlapping part to make the final product look like the following illustration.

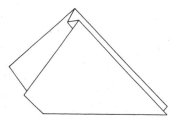

This is the ramp on which you can roll a marble.

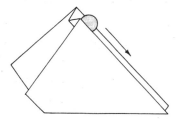

Place a marble on the groove of the ramp as in the illustration, and let it roll. The marble will roll down the ramp and away on the floor. Now, place the ramp on a carpeted floor. Roll a marble from the top of the ramp. Measure the distance from the ramp to the spot where the marble stopped. Record this distance on the following chart. Repeat the activity twice. Record these distances on the chart. Add the three measurements and divide by three. The quotient is the average distance. Record the average distance on the chart.

On Carpeted Floor	
No. times	cm
1	
2	
3	
Average	**cm**

On Wooden Floor	
No. times	cm
1	
2	
3	
Average	**cm**

Place the ramp on a wooden or linoleum floor. Place a marble at the same place on the ramp. Let the marble roll down. Measure the distance that the marble travels on the floor. Record the distance on the following chart. Repeat the activity twice. Find the average distance the marble travels on the hard floor.

Showy Science

How does this work?

When you placed the marble on the ramp, gravity made it roll down. When the marble hit the floor, it kept rolling. Once a marble starts rolling, it tends to keep rolling. Scientists have named this tendency *inertia*. Inertia is also described by Newton's first law of motion.

Inertia can be explained as: an object in motion stays in motion unless a force is applied to the object. If no force acts on a moving object, the object will keep moving at the same speed and in the same direction. A marble supposedly stays in one place if no other forces move it. However, by definition, a rolling marble will roll forever if no forces stop it. What forces stopped your moving marble?

The marble travels for a much shorter distance on the carpeted floor than on the non-carpeted floor. Why?

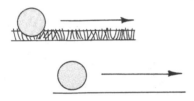

The marble that is rolling over the carpet contacts more materials in its path than the marble rolling on the hard floor as in the illustration. The carpet materials resist the marble's motion more than the hard floor. This resisting force on a moving object by contact is called *friction*. Therefore, the marble rolls for a longer distance on a hard floor than on a carpet because the wooden floor has less friction.

What other factors make the rolling marble stop? Some air friction is a factor. If you throw a marble into space without gravity or friction, do you think it will keep moving forever? Yes, once a spacecraft escapes the friction of the earth's atmosphere, no more power is needed to keep the craft moving. Revolving planets around the sun do not need power to keep moving either.

With the ramp and rolling marble, you can play games applying the concept of inertia.

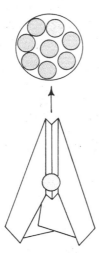

Make a circle on the floor. Place some marbles in the circle. Players aim a marble on the ramp and shoot it. The moving marble will hit the marbles. When the marbles are hit this way, some of them will move out of the circle. The person who rolled the single marble gets to keep all the marbles knocked out of the circle. Take turns rolling the single marble. The person who has the most marbles when the last marble is knocked out of the circle wins.

A Gravity-Powered Race Car

By using a rolling marble, you can race a paper car on a race track made from your desk top or classroom floor. Since you know the moving car stops by friction, you can make a friction-efficient car. This activity is fun for large groups.

This is a contest of creative ideas to make a friction-efficient paper car. Before you design your own creative car, make a sample paper car to learn how to race the cars.

For this activity, you need:

○ a piece of paper or an index card
○ transparent tape
○ a pair of scissors

To do this activity:

Cut the paper into a rectangle 8 by 12 centimeters. Fold the longer 12 centimeters in half as in the illustration. Snip off the upper and lower edges of one corner of the rectangle as in the illustration.

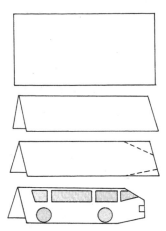

Bend the remainder of the cut edge inward, and tape the two pieces together (or you can staple them). This is your sample paper car to decorate.

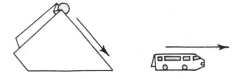

Here are some other examples of paper cars:

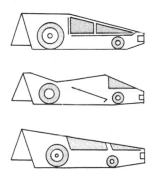

Place the paper car in front of the launching ramp. Place a marble on the ramp and let it go. The marble will roll down the ramp and into the car. Then the marble will push the car forward until friction stops it. Try this several times. Then all participants can design their own friction-efficient cars. Everyone can make their own cars, drive them, measure the distances, and determine the car that travels farthest. Study that car and find out why it traveled the longest distance.

Magic Tricks

Did you ever drop a coin into a glass by flicking a card? You can do it. You can even pull out a tablecloth without disturbing the objects on it.

For this activity, you need:

- ○ a coin
- ○ an index card
- ○ a drinking glass
- ○ a tablecloth
- ○ a two-liter pop bottle

To do this activity:

Place an index card on top of a glass. Place a coin on the index card as in the illustration. Make a circle with your index finger and thumb, and flick your index finger to knock the index card from the top of the glass. The coin will drop into the glass.

Why does this happen?

The coin at rest stays at rest unless a force is applied to the coin. The friction between the index card and the coin when the card was moved was not enough to overcome inertia. Therefore, the coin dropped into the glass. If you use sandpaper instead of an index card in this activity, the coin may not drop into the glass because the friction was large enough to overcome the inertia.

To do a similar activity:

Place a handkerchief on a corner of a table. Place a plastic cup half-full of water on the handkerchief as shown. Hold the other corner of the handkerchief and snap it out from under the glass. The cup will remain on the table without spilling.

From *Showy Science* published by GoodYearBooks. Copyright ©1994 by Hy Kim.

Showy Science

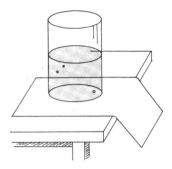

Seat Belts and Flying Drivers

This is a demonstration showing how inertia affects a moving car. It also demonstrates the importance of wearing seat belts in a moving vehicle.

For this activity, you need:

○ a toy truck or car
○ a doll that can sit in the truck or car, as shown

To do this activity:

Sit the doll in the car seat and run the car into a wall. Watch what happens to the doll. The doll will fly out of the car and toward the wall.

Why does this happen?

When the car moved, the doll moved with it. When the car crashed into the wall, the doll was still moving forward. As a result, the doll flew out of the car.

Try the activity again.

This time, tape the doll in the car seat. The tape, representing a seat belt, will hold the doll in the car when it crashes into the wall.

Remove the tape from the doll. With another car or a piece of wood, quickly hit the back of the car. What happens to the doll? The doll falls or flies backward out of the car.

Why does this happen?

The doll rested on its seat when the car was pushed quickly from behind. Inertia kept the doll in its motionless position, but the car jerked forward. As a result, the doll fell back or flew out of the car, depending on the power of the crash's impact.

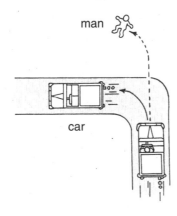

man

car

To do a similar activity:

Place the doll in the car seat without a seat belt. Move the car quickly, making a sharp left turn. What happens to the doll? The doll flew forward as the car made a sharp turn.

Try the activity again.

Make a sharp right turn this time. The doll will fly in the direction that the car was heading before it turned.

Why does this happen?

The definition of inertia is: The force acting on an object in motion, which stays in motion in a straight line unless a force is applied to the object.

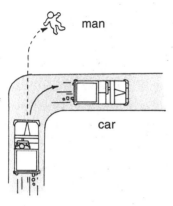

man

car

If no force acts on a moving object, the object will keep going at the same speed and in the same direction. You can explain the reason the doll flew out of the car by using the concept of inertia.

The Rolling Coffee Can

If you roll a coffee can away, you can make it roll back to you at your command.

For this activity, you need:

- ○ an empty coffee can
- ○ rubber bands
- ○ two or three large metal nuts
- ○ two paper clips
- ○ a tool to make holes in the can

To do this activity:

Stretch the rubber bands across the can from bottom to top. If they are too tightly stretched, connect two or three together. Combine three or four rubber band strings into one string if the rubber band is thin. Tie two or three metal nuts to the middle of the rubber band string with another rubber band as in the illustration.

Have an adult make a hole in the bottom of the can and another in the cap.

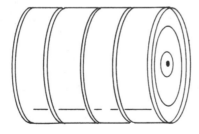

Thread one end of the rubber band through the hole in the bottom of the can. Secure the end by making a bolt from a paper clip. Stretch the other end of the rubber band through the hole in the cap. Secure the end by making another paper clip pin. Cap the can. The nuts and rubber strings are secured inside of the can as in the following illustration.

From *Showy Science* published by GoodYearBooks. Copyright ©1994 by Hy Kim.

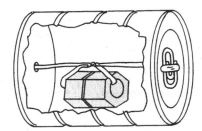

Now you are ready to perform the rolling can trick.

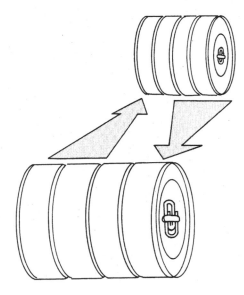

On a table top or hard floor, gently roll the can. The can will roll forward, stop, and roll back. Repeat the activity, pushing the can harder each time. Find the maximum distance that the can rolls back. If you push very hard, the can will not roll back. When you perform for other people, push the can just hard enough for it to roll back. When the can stops rolling forward, command the can to roll back.

Why does this work?

When the can rolled forward, the weight inside the can was not rolling. As a result, the rubber band was twisted as the can rolled forward. When the can stopped, the uncoiling rubber band made the can roll back.

A Pop Bottle Rocket

This activity will show you some of the scientific concepts that are applied to real rockets. The following activities will help you build a "pop bottle full of cloud," which will help you understand and interpret the process of cloud formation. However, this pop bottle rocket system is relatively hard to make.

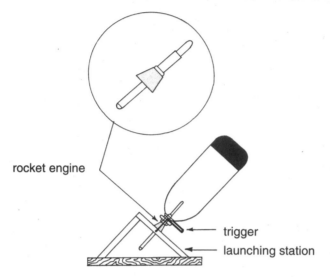

rocket engine

trigger

launching station

Three sections make up the rocket: engine, launching station, and trigger.

1. The Engine

To make a rocket engine, you need:

- ❍ an adult helper
- ❍ a used plastic ball-point pen
- ❍ scissors
- ❍ a size 7 rubber stopper with a hole (A wine cork works in place of the rubber stopper.)
- ❍ elastic rubber tubing with the same diameter as the ball-point pen
- ❍ a rubber band

To do this activity:

The first illustration on the next page shows plastic tubing from a used ball-point pen. The tubing is hollow. Have an adult seal the hole at the top of the tubing by heating and pressing the upper rim together.

As shown in the second illustration, cut away or file off a "u" shape on one side of the top part so that air can pass through the u-shaped cut.

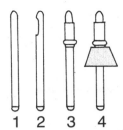

1 2 3 4

Cover the cut area with soft rubber tubing and secure the inner end with a rubber band. The rubber tubing serves as a one-way valve in the engine.

Insert the plastic tubing through the hole of a rubber stopper as in the illustration. Your rocket engine is complete.

The rubber stopper seals the air when the opening of the pop bottle is pushed down on the stopper. When air is pumped into the bottle, the rubber valve will allow air to come in but stop air from leaking out, keeping high air pressure in the bottle rocket.

2.The Launching Station

To build a launching station, you need:

○ scrap wood
○ an adult helper
○ a drill
○ your rocket engine

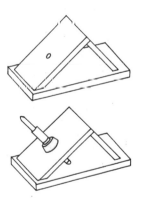

To do this activity:

Using some scrap wood, make a launching station as the illustration. A wide base panel makes the station more stable. A piece of 1' x 2' lumber is convenient for the upper part of the station. Have an adult drill a hole in the middle of the engine panel as in the illustration. Install the engine through the hole as in the illustration. You may secure the engine to the panel with rubber caulking or liquid nail. The launching panel is complete.

3. The Trigger

To make the trigger, you need:

- ○ an adult helper
- ○ a coat hanger
- ○ pliers
- ○ a tool to drill a hole

To do this activity:

This is what a trigger looks like:

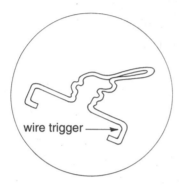

wire trigger →

The trigger is a safety device that keeps the inflated bottle on the launching station. Look at the illustration below. See where the trigger is located on your rocket launcher. Have an adult drill holes in the wood, one on either side, as shown below. Insert the ends of the trigger in the holes in the wood.

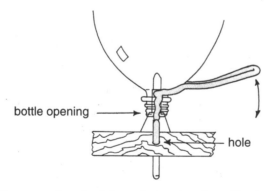

bottle opening →

hole

The round end of the trigger is a handle that you pull or push to launch the rocket. The pop bottle has a round ring around it. Bend the wire as in the illustration so that when you place the trigger on the neck of a pop bottle on the engine, the ring can be caught by the trigger. Measure the lengths of the lower part of the trigger and cut off the excess length. Bend the ends. Have an adult drill holes on the side of the engine panel. Insert the ends of the trigger. When you pull the trigger, the pop bottle rocket is freed from the engine.

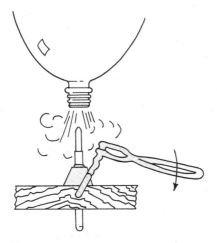

Now you have completed the rocket system and are ready to launch it. You can demonstrate many difficult scientific concepts with this rocket. Use your rocket to do the following activities.

Count Down, Blast Off!

For this activity, you need:

❍ your rocket system
❍ an air pump (the kind you use to fill your bicycle tire)

To do this activity:

Take your rocket system and an air pump to an open field or a large room. Press the opening of the bottle to the stopper of the engine until the bottle stands by itself. Without putting the trigger on the ring of the bottle neck, pump air into the bottle. Count the number of pumps it takes until the rocket launches by itself. At the point where the air pressure exerts more force than the force that holds the bottle on the stopper, the bottle rocket will blast off. Add one or two more pumps to the number required without the trigger. This is about the right number of pumps for blast off.

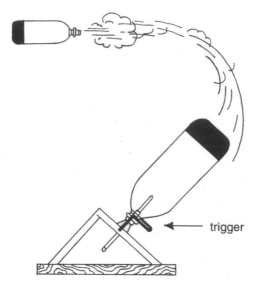

trigger

Set the trigger, pump air into the rocket, count down, and then pull the trigger. Blast off! How far did it go? How can you launch the rocket so it lands far away from the launching station? You may launch it from different angles. Do not launch it straight upward at a 180 degree angle because it may land near you. Can you aim your rocket at a target?

How does this work?

When you pull the trigger, the air compressed inside the bottle will rush out through its opening. The air rushing out the back of the bottle exerts an action-reaction force on the bottle. The rocket travels because of this opposite push. A great scientist named Isaac Newton did many experiments and discovered this law: "For every action there is an equal and opposite reaction." What are "action" and "reaction" in your rocket operation?

The Water Engine

For this activity, you need:

- ○ your rocket system
- ○ a pail of water
- ○ plenty of open space

To do this activity:

Take the rocket system and a pail of water to an open space. Using water, you can make your rocket quite powerful and send it a long distance. Fill about one-third of the bottle with water and insert the stopper of the engine into the opening of the bottle. Set up the trigger and the rocket system in the launching position. Because the bottle is heavy with water, you may have to hold the bottle or lean it against an object. Pump air into the bottle and launch the rocket. What happened to the water? Why does the rocket travel such a long distance?

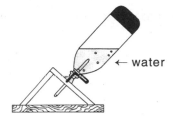
← water

You may want to find out what amount of water in the bottle makes the rocket travel the longest distance by adjusting the amount of water each time.

Why do water engines travel further than air engines in pop bottle rockets?

There is more push in the water engine than in the air engine. The product of the mass and velocity of a body is called its *momentum*. The momentum of reaction depends on the momentum of action. If the momentum of action increases, the momentum of reaction also increases because of the law of conservation of momentum. In the water engine, the momentum of action, which is the mass of the water multiplied by the velocity of the water pushed out, is much greater than the momentum of action of air in the air rocket. The momentum of action in the water engine is the mass of the compressed air multiplied by the velocity of the air. Therefore, the momentum of the water engine rocket is greater than that of the air engine rocket.

In order to send the rocket the longest distance using the water engine, the amount of water in the rocket should be equal to the amount that is completely pushed out of the bottle by the compressed air pressure while the rocket travels. In a real rocket, fuels are burned, making hot gases that are pushed out for a much longer length of time than your rocket.

The Cloud Machine

For this activity, you need:

○ your rocket system
○ water
○ an air pump

To do this activity:

Add a small amount of water (preferably warm) to the pop bottle. Press the opening of the bottle to the stopper of the engine. Pump air as you did to launch the rocket (see illustration). Hold the bottle with one hand, and pull the trigger with the other hand. Observe the bottle. You will have a bottleful of cloud! If you squeeze the bottle, some of the cloud will be squeezed out. If you launch the rocket and pick it up when it lands, you will probably find the same result: a bottleful of cloud.

You can clear out the cloud completely. To do so, place the bottle of cloud on the launching station, and pump air into the bottle again. Like magic, the cloud will disappear!

Why does this work?

It is much easier to demonstrate than to explain. After you compressed the air in the bottle, invisible water vapor was still present in the bottle. By pulling the trigger, you released air from the bottle, lowering the air pressure. As a result, the temperature cooled. The invisible water vapor in the bottle of compressed air condensed and became many small water drops. A cloud is made of water drops like these.

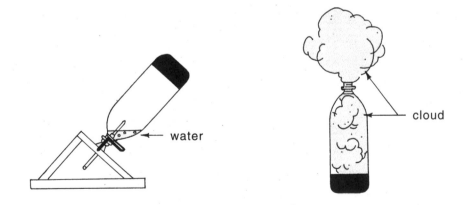

water

cloud

In nature, many kinds of clouds are formed the same way: warm, moist air rises to an area of lower air pressure. The air expands and cools, making the vapor condense into clouds.

From *Showy Science* published by GoodYearBooks. Copyright ©1994 by Hy Kim.

A Balloon Rocket

Balloon rocket activities are more fun if you and your audience participate as team members. The balloon rocket launched in this demonstration will travel from earth to a newly created moon about fifty yards away.

For this activity, each group needs:

○ a giant cylindrical balloon that inflates to four feet
○ two paper clips
○ one piece of tubing
○ two long pieces of string

To do this activity:

Group your audience into teams and let each team select a name. The teams are companies that manufacture rockets that travel to the moon.

To construct the rocket, have each team complete the following procedures:

1. Insert the tubing in the open end of the balloon. Tie it tightly with 15 to 25 centimeters of string.

2. Tie a paper clip at the other end of the string as shown.

3. Pinch the closed end of the balloon and tie it with a second piece of string.

4. Tie a paper clip to the end of the second piece of string.

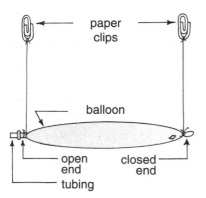

The rocket is ready for launching. Have each team inflate their balloon. Stretch the string from the earth (you) to the moon (fifty yards away). While holding the mouth of the inflated balloon closed, have a team member hook the balloon to the string with paper clips so that the closed end faces the moon as in the next illustration. Count down from ten to zero. Launch the balloon by releasing it.

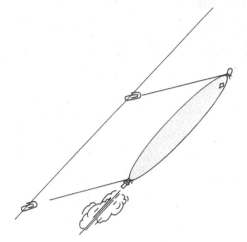

The rocket will move toward the moon. If the rocket does not make it to the moon, let the team work on it to discover why. Variables that usually cause trouble are the length of the string between the paper clips and the balloon and the size of the tubing. By experimenting, let the teams find out how to get the best performance by varying the length of the string and the size of the tubing.

Why does this work?

Air rushed out of the balloon after you released it. As a reaction to the rushing air, the balloon rocket moved in the opposite direction. If the air pushes harder, the rocket travels further. This principle is Newton's third law of motion: "For every action there is an equal and opposite reaction." Using this principle, scientists operate jet planes and rockets.

From *Showy Science* published by GoodYearBooks. Copyright ©1994 by Hy Kim.

Will Water Spill From an Upside-Down Cup?

If you flip over a cup of water, water falls out of the cup. But does water spill from an upside-down cup?

For this activity, you need:

- ○ a paper cup
- ○ water
- ○ one meter of string
- ○ a nail

To do this activity:

Poke two holes near the rim of a paper cup. Tie a string through the holes as in the illustration. Fill the cup two-thirds full with water.

Holding the other end of the string, whirl the cup around the side of your body so the cup flies in a vertical circle.

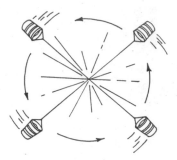

If you look at the cup when it is on the top of the circle, the cup is upside-down, but water does not spill.

Why does this happen?

The inertia of the moving water is greater than the force of gravity on the water. As a result, the water stays in the cup. This is the inertia that keeps people in a roller coaster when the cars are upside down in the loops.

The Moon's Orbit of Earth

The moon revolves around the earth. Earth and other planets revolve around the sun. You can demonstrate the moon's orbit of the earth.

For this activity, you need:

○ a Ping-Pong ball
○ a tennis ball or a baseball
○ string
○ tape
○ a wooden spool
○ a large paper clip

To do this activity:

Tape one end of a 50-centimeter string to a Ping-Pong ball. Tape the string about 15 centimeters from the Ping-Pong ball to the baseball as in the illustration.

From *Showy Science* published by GoodYearBooks. Copyright ©1994 by Hy Kim.

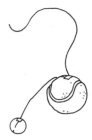

Hold the other end of the string between your palms. Spin the string by rubbing your palms together. Watch the balls. The Ping-Pong ball will revolve around the baseball.

To do a related activity:

If you have a wooden spool and a large paper clip, you can make another spinning device.

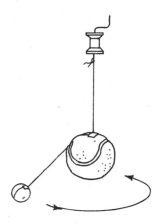

Stretch and bend the paper clip as shown in the illustration. Insert one end of the paper clip wire to the hole in the spool. Make a hook at the end of the wire. Tie the end of the string that is taped to the balls to the hook. Hold the spool with one hand. Turn the paper clip handle.

How does this work?

The centripetal force, which is gravity in this case, causes this revolution to occur. The moon revolves around the earth and the earth and other planets revolve around the sun the same way.

The Phases of the Moon

Why does the moon experience phases? Why does the moon wax and wane? You can demonstrate the phases of the moon in your living room or in your classroom using the following simple procedures.

For this activity, you need:

○ a basketball
○ a flashlight or film projector
○ some assistants

To do this activity:

Designate one person as the sun. He or she stays in one spot holding a flashlight or film projector light. The sun's job is to shine the light beam directly on the moon that is revolving around the earth. Designate one person as the moon carrier. The moon carrier carries the basketball (the moon) along the moon's orbit as shown in the illustration. Let the other people be moon watchers on earth. The moon watchers sit on the earth.

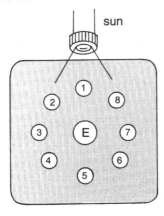
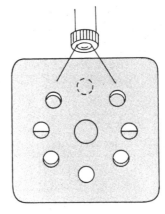

Darken the room and let the moon carrier revolve around the moon's orbit while the sunlight follows it.

From *Showy Science* published by GoodYearBooks. Copyright ©1994 by Hy Kim.

More information about moon phases:

From the earth, we can only see the moon's surface that reflects the sunlight. When the moon is located between the sun and earth, we face the shaded part of the moon. Therefore, we do not see it. We call this a new moon. Then the following moons appear in sequence: crescent moon, half moon, gibbous moon, full moon, gibbous moon, half moon, crescent moon, and new moon. It takes a month to complete this moon phase cycle. The planet Venus also appears in different phases according to the time of the year.

What Force Keeps the Moon From Flying Away?

In the model of the moon's orbit of earth described in a previous activity, the string between the Ping-Pong ball and the baseball kept the revolving Ping-Pong ball from flying away by inertia. However, no string connects the earth and the moon or the sun and the planets. The moon travels about 2,000 miles per hour around the earth. What keeps the rushing moon in its regular orbit? You can demonstrate the answer.

For this activity, you need:

- ○ a Ping-Pong ball
- ○ one meter of string
- ○ a wooden spool
- ○ tape
- ○ a metal washer or small potato

To do this activity:

Tape one end of the string to a Ping-Pong ball. Thread the other end of the string through the hole of the spool. Tie a washer or small potato to the end of the string.

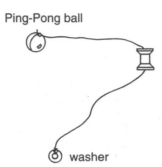

Ping-Pong ball

washer

Hold the spool and whirl the Ping-Pong ball while letting the washer hang under the spool.

Watch the washer's position as you slow down and speed up your whirling. If you speed up the whirling, the washer keeps going up until it touches the spool. If you slow down the speed of whirling, the washer keeps going down until the ball touches the spool.

How does this work?

Gravity between the moon and the earth balances the inertia of the orbiting moon. If the inertial force of the moon was greater than its gravitational force, then the moon would gradually fly away from the earth. On the other hand, if the inertial force was weaker than the gravitational force, then the moon would revolve more closely to the earth.

A Propeller-Powered Helicopter

The Wright brothers were fascinated by a toy propeller that flew up and away when they spun it. They kept spinning it to watch it fly. Later, they made a big propeller and attached it to a motor that would spin it. It was the first airplane. You can make a toy helicopter like the one with which the Wright Brothers played.

For this activity, you need:

○ an adult helper
○ a 15-centimeter piece of wood
○ a small dowel
○ a piece of wood, 15 cm long by 3 cm high by 3 cm wide
○ sandpaper
○ a drill
○ wood glue

To do this activity:

Have an adult help you sand the ends of the piece of wood so that the only part left unsanded is a 3 x 3 cm square in the middle of the wood.

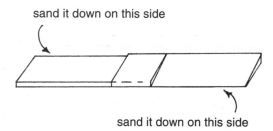

sand it down on this side

sand it down on this side

This will be your propeller. Sand both sides of the wood at each side of the propeller. Have an adult drill a hole in the middle of the propeller. Insert one end of the dowel into the hole and secure it with glue.

The toy helicopter is completed. After the glue dries, hold the dowel between your palms and spin the shaft counterclockwise. The helicopter will fly up and away!

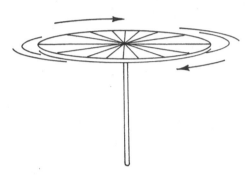

Be careful with the spinning blades of the helicopter. It could hurt someone if they hit him or her during flight. The Wright brothers made many helicopters and experimented with them before they put a engine-powered propeller in their airplane.

Why does the propeller work?

When the propeller turns, there is low pressure on the top of the blades. The higher pressure on the bottom of the blades forces the propeller up.

From *Showy Science* published by GoodYearBooks. Copyright ©1994 by Hy Kim.

A Paper Helicopter

Making a helicopter with a wooden propeller requires lots of work. A paper helicopter is much easier to make.

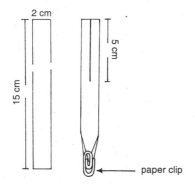

paper clip

For this activity, you need:

○ a piece of paper 15 cm by 2 cm
○ a paper clip

To do this activity:

Cut out a piece of paper measuring 15 centimeters by 2 centimeters as shown. Make a 5-centimeter slit in the top of the piece and fold the lower corners as shown. Secure a paper clip to the folded part of the strip.

Bend one half of the upper part in one direction and the other half in the opposite direction as shown in the side view of the paper strip. The helicopter is complete. Now, hold the helicopter by the paper clip with your thumb and index finger. Throw it up to the sky and watch the path of the helicopter.

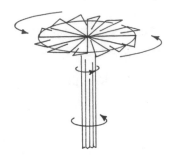

It will dash and fall, spinning like a helicopter.

Why does it spin?

When the helicopter fell, it passed through air. Half of one side of the blade is cut and the other side is bent. Air passes quickly over the cut side, but air passes more slowly over the bent side because the blade creates resistance. It is this imbalance of forces that causes the helicopter to spin.

A Paper Airplane

Did you ever make a paper airplane and fly it? You can fold a paper airplane many different ways. Only one easy way of folding a paper airplane is described here. After making your airplane, you can experiment with controlling it after it is launched. The principles that control a paper airplane are identical to those used in real airplanes.

For this activity, you need:

○ a piece of paper, 8 1/2" x 11"

To do this activity:

Fold a paper airplane following this sequence:

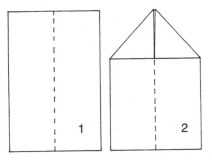

1. Make a crease in the paper as shown above. Do this by folding and unfolding the sheet along the center of the long side.

2. Fold the upper corners along the center crease.

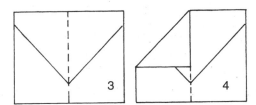

3. Fold the top triangular section over the lower part as shown. Make sure the center lines meet the crease. They should overlap the rectangular part of the paper about 2 centimeters.

4. Fold the left upper corner as shown above. Also fold the right corner as shown in illustration 5.

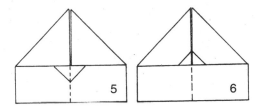

5. There will be a small triangular tip. Fold this tip upward as in illustration 6.

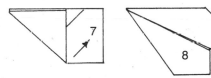

6. Fold the pentagonal shape backward along the center line as shown in illustration 7.

7. Fold the two trapezoidal shapes upward as in illustration 8.

8. Tape the two wings as shown in illustration 9. Now you have an airplane.

Hold the body of the plane, and throw the plane horizontally to launch it. The plane will fly.

rudder
↓

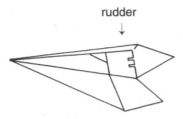

To control the plane, make a rudder by cutting two horizontal slits in the back of the plane as in the illustration. Bend the rudder slightly to the right. Turn over the plane and launch it. Watch how the plane flies.

How do you steer a plane?

You will notice that the plane turns right on its flight path if the rudder is turned right. The plane will turn left if the rudder is turned left. The part of the rudder turned to one side creates more air resistance than the other part. This makes the plane turn to the same side as the rudder is turned.

Square Puzzles

Some people love to solve puzzles. Do you? You can make challenging puzzles by using cardboard and scissors, then solve the puzzles yourself. These activities are excellent for individual use as well as in the classroom.

For these activies, each person needs:

○ construction paper or manila folders
○ a pair of scissors

To do these activities:

Cut out squares from construction paper. Cut the square into sections. For example, four-piece puzzles are shown in the illustration. Mix up the four pieces of a puzzle, then put them together into the original square. A puzzle can be made using curved cuts, straight cuts, or a combination of the two. The curved line puzzle is easier than the straight cut puzzle to solve, yet it is more difficult to cut along the curved line.

Start with a two-piece puzzle, then increase the number of cuts. Some sample puzzles are shown.

It may seem too easy a task to put the puzzle back together to form a square. However, you may make a five or six piece puzzle that you cannot easily put into the original square.

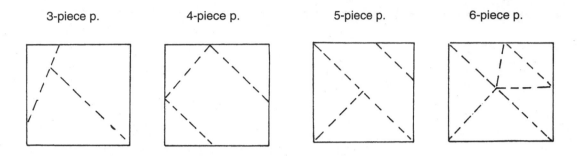

3-piece p.   4-piece p.   5-piece p.   6-piece p.

This activity is particularly challenging for group competition. Each group designs a puzzle with a certain number of pieces, then lets the other group solve the puzzle.

Tanagram

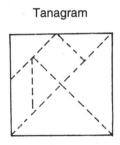

The tangram is a well-known seven-piece puzzle. Make a tangram, scramble the pieces, and put it together into a square. The color of the front of the square should be the same as the back of the square. This will make the puzzle more difficult than a puzzle made of construction paper having a different shaded color front and back.

If you cannot solve these more difficult puzzles, begin with easy ones and practice. Practice and experience will make you a better puzzle solver.

Clay Boat: Challenging Problems

The Clay Boat, an original unit of *Elementary School Science* (Selective Educational Equipment, 1969), provides many challenging problems to solve. Following are some activities that are variations of the Clay Boat. You can do the activities by yourself. However, doing them in groups of classmates may be more fun.

For these activities, you need:

○ modeling clay

○ centimeter rulers

○ a graduated cylinder or metric measuring cup

○ metric weighing scales

○ marbles or ceramic tiles

○ small jars

○ a bucket of water

How Do You Measure the Volume of a Lump of Clay?

Take out a lump of modeling clay. In what ways can you find its volume?

One way to measure the volume of irregular solid shapes is by water displacement.

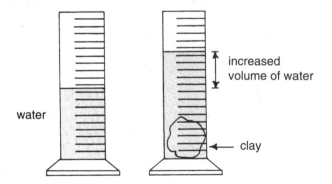

Put some water into a graduated cylinder. Measure the volume of the water. Then place the lump of clay into the water. The water level will increase by an amount equal to the volume of the clay. Measure the new volume of the water and clay. The difference between your first and second readings equals the volume of the clay.

From *Showy Science* published by GoodYearBooks. Copyright ©1994 by Hy Kim.

By this method, you can measure the volume of a potato, a nut, and many other objects.

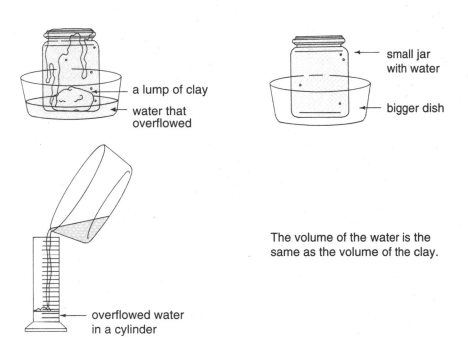

a lump of clay

water that overflowed

small jar with water

bigger dish

overflowed water in a cylinder

The volume of the water is the same as the volume of the clay.

If you do not have a big measuring cylinder, you can use the method shown above. Place a container full of water into a larger container. Put the lump of clay in the inner water-filled container. Water will overflow from this inner container. Measure the volume of overflow water by pouring it out of the outer container into a measuring cup. The measurement of the overflowed water equals the volume of the clay.

Another way to measure the volume of the lump of clay is by molding the clay into a geometric shape like a rectangular prism and then calculating its volume.

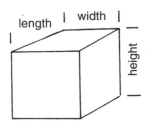

length   width

height

Activities for Exploring Gravity, Motion, and Other Forces

Pound the clay on the top of a table. Shape it into a rectangular prism. Then measure its length, width, and height with a centimeter ruler. Let's pretend that the length is 10 centimeters, the width is 10 centimeters, and the height is 15 centimeters. Find the volume of the clay by the following multiplication: 10 centimeters x 10 centimeters x 15 centimeters = 1,500 centimeters ^{3}, which is read "1500 cubic centimeters ^{3}". You can write "cubic centimeter" in its short form of "cc." 100 cc means 100 centimeters ^{3}. Also 1 centimeter^3 is the same as 1 milliliter (ml) in the metric system.

Why Is the Clay Lighter in Water Than in Air?

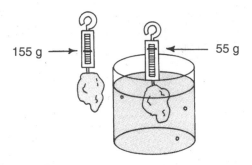

Measure a lump of clay with a spring scale. Read the weight as in the illustration. The scale reads 155 grams. Now, submerge the clay completely underwater while holding the scale as shown. The scale reads only 55 grams! Where did the 100 grams go? Is everything lighter in water than in air? If so, why? In order to find the answers, do the following activity.

Give each group a weight scale with gram units. Let them measure the weight of their lump of clay. Record their results in a chart similar to the one below.

GROUP	1	2	3	4
Volume of the clay:	100cc	350cc	500cc	260cc
Weight in air:	155g	543g	775g	403g
Weight in water:	55g	193g	275g	137g
Weight difference	100g	350g	500g	266g
Water displaced	100cc	350cc	500cc	260cc

The data in the chart were collected during actual class activities. Each group had an assignment to measure a certain amount of clay by the water displacement method. For example, the first group measured 100 cc of clay by repeatedly dropping it in small amounts into a water-filled cylinder until the water level increased to 100 cc. Then they took out the clay and molded it into a lump. In the same way, the second group measured 350 cc, the third group 500 cc, and the fourth group 260 cc.

Each group weighed their clay in the air and in the water. Then they calculated the weight differences between the air and water methods. Look at Group 1's data. Read the volume of the clay, the weight difference, and the amount of water displaced. Do you find a pattern?

One cc of cold water weighs one gram. 100 cc of clay submerged in water displaces 100 cc of water. 100 c of displaced water buoys up the clay with 100 grams of force. Thus the clay weighs less in water.

More than 2,000 years ago, Archimedes discovered this principle: An object submerged in water is pushed up with a force that equals the weight of the displaced water. This law is called *Archimedes' principle*.

By using this principle, which says that the weight difference between an object in air and in water equals the weight of the displaced water, you can solve the following problems:

Problem 1:

You have a lump of clay that has a volume of 1000 cc and weighs 1700 grams in air. How much does this lump weigh in water? Solution: 1700-1000 = 700. It will weigh 700 grams in water.

Problem 2:

You have a rock that has a volume of 5000 cc and weighs 14 kg (14,000 g) in air. How much does the rock weigh in water?

Problem 3:

You have a dog that weighs 40 kg (40,000 g) in air and 0 g in water. What is the dog's volume?

Because of the constant ratio between the weight of a lump of clay in air and the weight of an equal amount of water, scientists discovered the *specific gravity* of substances. Specific gravity is found by dividing the weight of an object by the weight of an equal volume of water. The specific gravity of a substance is a number that tells how many times as dense the substance is compared to water. Some substances' specific gravities are: water, 1; this activity's modeling clay, 1.55; diamond, 3.5; gold, 19.3; ice, 0.92; human body, 1.07; copper, 8.9; and oak wood, 0.85.

These specific gravities help solve many mysteries. For example, if you question the purity of a 500 g gold bracelet, you can analyze its degree of purity by using specific gravity. The specific gravity of pure gold is 19.3. Let " x " equal the same amount of water. The problem would be written as $500 \div x = 19.3$. Figuring this out, you discover that $x = 25.91$. Now, measure the volume of the bracelet. If the volume equals 25.91 cc, then the bracelet is pure gold. If the bracelet is made of 450 g pure gold and 50 g copper, the total weight is 500 g, but the volume is 28.94 cc ($450 \div x = 19.3$, $x = 23.32$; $50 \div y = 8.9$, $y = 5.62$; $x+y = 28.94$). By this method, Archimedes solved the problem that his king asked him to solve. The problem was to find out whether the silversmith cheated when using gold to make a crown.

Can You Make the Lump of Clay Float?

Make a boat with clay. Launch it on a surface of water. For group activities, let each group of students measure 100 cc of modeling clay. Have them make a boat that floats in a bucket of water.

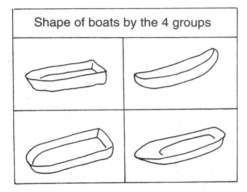

Shape of boats by the 4 groups

Draw a chart like the one illustrated below on a piece of paper or on the chalkboard. Let each group of students measure and record their data on the chart.

The data in this chart were collected from an actual activity.

GROUP	Volume of clay	Weight of clay in air	Water displaced
1	100cc	155g	155cc
2	100cc	155g	155cc
3	100cc	155g	155cc
4	100cc	155g	155cc

To measure the amount of water displaced by launching the boat, collect overflowing water with a wide-mouthed container. Measure this amount by pouring it into a graduated cylinder. Each group will discover that, regardless of their shape, boats that weigh 155 g will displace 155 cc of water. This equals the weight of the clay.

Why does a lump of clay with a volume of 100 cc displace 100 cc of water when submerged in water, but a clay boat displaces 155 cc, which equals the weight of the clay?

Mysterious, isn't it? In order to float, the volume of the boat must be greater than the volume of the displaced water. The shape and size of the boat does not change the volume of displaced water. The weight of the displaced water always equals the weight of the clay.

Loading Cargo in the Boat

Load marbles into the clay boat until the boat sinks. Let each group reshape the boat without adding more clay so that the boat can carry as much as possible. Record the number of marbles that each boat can carry. Find the weight of each marble by weighing ten marbles in a container. Then measure the weight of the empty container and subtract it from the first measurement. Divide this number by ten, and this is the weight of one marble. Find the total cargo weight of each boat by multiplying the number of marbles in the boat by the weight of each marble.

A boat with a large volume can carry more cargo. The weight of the displaced water always equals the weight of the boat and its cargo. For example, if a boat weighs 155 g and its cargo weighs 140 g, the boat will displace 295 g (295 cc) of water. Therefore, the volume of the boat must be larger than 295 cc. This concept leads to the following activities.

How Many Marbles Can a Cup Hold on the Surface of Water?

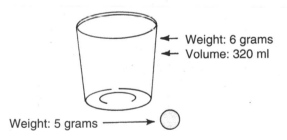

Weight: 6 grams
Volume: 320 ml

Weight: 5 grams

Measure the weights and volumes of thin plastic cups or paper cups. The volumes can be estimated by measuring how much water the cups hold. For example, the weight of a plastic cup is 6 g and its volume (capacity) is 320 cc.

If one marble weighs 5 g, how many marbles can the plastic cup hold while floating on water?

Solution: Let the number of marbles = M. 5 g x M + 6 g = 320 grams. 5 g x M = 314 grams. Therefore, M= $\frac{314 \text{ g}}{5 \text{ g}}$) and M = 62.8 marbles. So the container will hold 62 marbles while floating on water.

Measure the weight and volume of a glass. Predict how many marbles the glass can hold while floating on water. You can repeat this activity with many different containers.

A Penny Barge

This is an exciting and challenging activity for groups of students. This activity can be part of the clay boat activity as well as an independent activity.

For this activity, you need:

- ○ aluminum foil
- ○ scissors
- ○ about one hundred pennies
- ○ a pan of water

To do this activity:

Ask each individual or team of two to cut out a 15 x 15 centimeter aluminum foil square. Ask each team to make a barge on which to load pennies.

After each team completes their barge, let a team member load pennies onto the barge, one at a time, until the barge sinks in the water.

With the same size of aluminum foil, they can rebuild their barge as many times as they wish to improve the cargo capacity. Set a time limit. The team that makes the barge which holds the most pennies is the winner.

One way to analyze the building of a barge that can load the largest numbers of pennies is to maximize the capacity of the barge.

From *Showy Science* published by GoodYearBooks. Copyright ©1994 by Hy Kim.

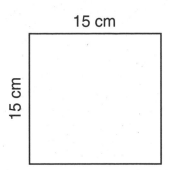

15 cm

15 cm

If you fold the edges for 3 centimeters depth to make a rectangular-shaped barge, the width of the barge is 9 centimeters (15 centimeters - 3 centimeters - 3 centimeters = 9 centimeters), and the capacity (volume) of the barge is 243 cubic centimeters (9 centimeters x 9 centimeters x 3 centimeters = 243 centimeters ^{3}).

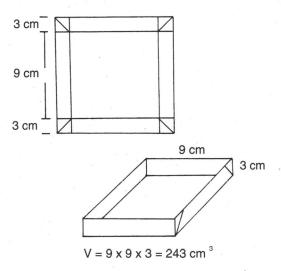

3 cm

9 cm

3 cm

9 cm

3 cm

$V = 9 \times 9 \times 3 = 243$ cm^3

If you make a barge by folding the edges for 1 centimeters depth, which is centimeters ^{3} the height of the barge, then the capacity of the barge is 169 centimeters ^{3} (13 x 13 x 1=169). If you extend the height of the barge to the heights in the table, you will obtain the following capacities for the barge:

Height	Capacity	
1 cm	13 centimeters x 13 centimeters x 1 centimeters	= **169** centimeters ^{3}
2 cm	11 centimeters x 11 centimeters x 2 centimeters	= **242** centimeters ^{3}
2.5 cm	10 centimeters x 10 centimeters x 2.5 centimeters	= **250** centimeters ^{3}
3 cm	9 centimeters x 9 centimeters x 3 centimeters	= **243** centimeters ^{3}
4 cm	7 centimeters x 7 centimeters x 4 centimeters	= **196** centimeters ^{3}
5 cm	5 centimeters x 5 centimeters x 5 centimeters	= **125** centimeters ^{3}

As shown in the table, whoever made the barge with 2.5 centimeters sides can load the most pennies.

ACTIVITIES FOR
EXPLORING
EARTH

Day and Night

We have been experiencing day and night since time began. Long ago, some people believed that a sun god traveled across the heavens from east to west, bringing light and darkness. In this activity, you will demonstrate how day and night actually occur.

For this activity, you need:

○ a globe or ball

○ a flashlight (If you demonstrate it in a classroom, you will need a film projector light in place of a flashlight. Do not use a regular lamp because its light brightens the whole room; you will not be able to see the shadows on the globe clearly.)

To do this activity:

Darken the room. Shine the light directly onto the globe as shown. You can see that one-half of the globe reflects the light and the other half is shaded. The shaded part represents nighttime and the bright part daytime.

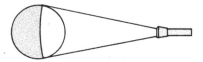

If you rotate the globe on its axis, night and day both shift to other parts of the globe.

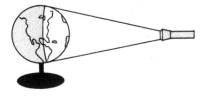

It takes 24 hours for the earth to complete its rotation, making the day light and the night dark.

From *Showy Science* published by GoodYearBooks. Copyright ©1994 by Hy Kim.

Showy Science

Clockwise or Counterclockwise?

Let's listen to a pretend argument between a person from the Southern Hemisphere and a person from the Northern Hemisphere. The northerner insists that the earth rotates on its axis counterclockwise, and the southerner disagrees, saying that the earth rotates clockwise. Can you settle this argument?

For this activity, you need:

○ a globe or ball

To do this activity:

On your globe, mark the North Pole, the South Pole, and the United States. Mark Washington, DC and San Francisco as in the illustration.

San Francisco   Washington D.C.

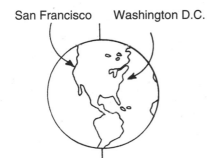

Rotate the globe clockwise on its axis. See whether Washington, DC or San Francisco comes into the light first. The morning light comes first to San Francisco. We know that this does not actually happen because the sun travels east to west in our country. San Francisco is further west than Washington, DC. Therefore, the earth does not rotate clockwise.

Rotate the globe counterclockwise. Notice that Washington, DC gets the light first. We know the sun rises first in Washington, DC. The earth must rotate counter-clockwise. The person from the Northern Hemisphere is correct!

North Pole

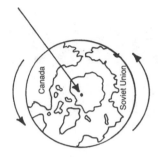

However, the counterclockwise rotation theory is correct if you look at the earth from the North Pole. The same rotation looks different from the South Pole, as demonstrated in the following activity.

South Pole

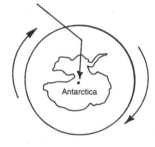

Mark the South Pole in the middle of Antarctica. Look at the North Pole and rotate the globe counterclockwise. Keep rotating the globe counterclockwise and look at the globe from the South Pole. Which direction is the globe rotating? Clockwise! By observing the rotation from the South Pole, you can say that the southerner's claim is correct and the northerner's incorrect.

Can you ever correctly settle this argument?

The earth rotates in one direction, but this direction looks different from different points on the globe. Both answers are correct—it depends on your perspective!

From *Showy Science* published by GoodYearBooks. Copyright ©1994 by Hy Kim.

What Makes Seasons?

Some parts of the world have four seasons, some do not. This activity will demonstrate the reason for the four seasons.

For this activity, you need:

○ a globe or ball

To do this activity:

First, identify the equator and the axis on the globe. Find the Tropic of Cancer and the Tropic of Capricorn. They are parallel to the equator. Spin the tilted globe on its axis as shown. The earth's axis is tilted at 23.5°.

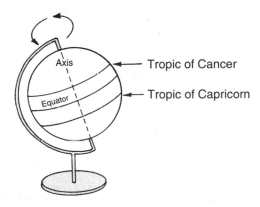

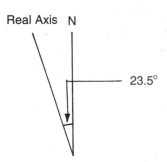

This tilt of the axis causes the seasons.

From *Showy Science* published by GoodYearBooks. Copyright ©1994 by Hy Kim.

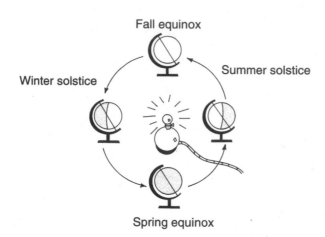

Fall equinox

Winter solstice

Summer solstice

Spring equinox

Place a lighted lamp on the floor or on a large table. Tilt the globe on its axis and place it near the light. Move the globe along a circular path around the lamp. Rotate the globe on its axis as shown.

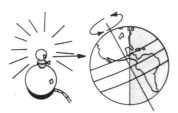

Summer solstice: June 21

Set the globe on the Summer Solstice position. Spin the globe on its axis. Among the lines of the Tropic of Cancer, the equator, and the Tropic of Capricorn, which line receives the direct light? Because the axis is tilted 23.5° toward the light, the Tropic of Cancer, which is 23.5° latitude north, receives vertical sunshine. As a result, the Northern Hemisphere, half of the earth north of the equator, receives more of the sun's energy than the Southern Hemisphere. Summer begins on Summer Solstice in the Northern Hemisphere. Winter begins in the Southern Hemisphere on the same day.

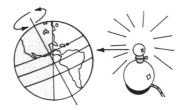

Winter Solstice: December 21

Set the globe on the Winter Solstice position. Spin the globe on its axis. On which of the three lines does the light shine directly? The sun shines vertically on the Tropic of

From *Showy Science* published by GoodYearBooks. Copyright ©1994 by Hy Kim.

Capricorn. The southern tip of the axis is tilted 23.5° toward the sun. The Tropic of Capricorn, which is 23.5° latitude south, receives the vertical sunshine. On Winter Solstice, December 21, winter begins in the Northern Hemisphere. Summer begins in the Southern Hemisphere on the same day.

Fall equinox: September 22

Set the globe on the Fall Equinox position. Spin the globe on its axis. On which of the three lines does the sun directly shine? Even if the axis is tilted sideways, the equator receives the vertical light. Both hemispheres receive equal amounts of the sun's energy on Fall Equinox, which is September 22. This day marks the beginning of fall in the Northern Hemisphere and of spring in the Southern Hemisphere.

Spring equinox: March 21

Set the globe on the Spring Equinox position. Spin the globe on its axis. On which line does the sun shine vertically? Even if the axis is tilted sideways, the equator receives the vertical light. Both hemispheres receive equal amounts of the sun's energy on Spring Equinox, which is March 21. On this day, spring starts in the Northern Hemisphere and fall starts in the Southern Hemisphere.

Is the Earth Closer to the Sun in Summer or Winter?

In another argument, the first person says the earth is closer to the sun during the winter than the summer. The second person says the earth is the same distance from the sun in both seasons. The third person says the earth is closer to the sun in the summer than in the winter. Who is correct? You can settle this argument with a simple calculation.

For this activity, you need:

○ a calculator

To do this activity:

First, familiarize yourself with this diagram:

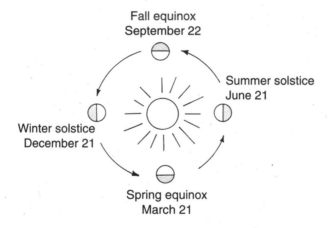

One way to judge the distance between the sun and the earth in winter and in summer is to calculate the number of days the earth takes to travel around the sun. Since the weather, temperatures, and degree of slant toward the sun in the Spring and Fall Equinoxes are about the same, we can assume that the distances between the sun and the earth are the same. Since the argument concerns the distance between the sun and the earth during the summer and winter, we can calculate the number of days the earth travels from the Fall Equinox to the Spring Equinox. We can compare that to the number of days the earth travels from the Spring Equinox to the Fall Equinox. If both numbers are equal, then we can assume that the distances between

From *Showy Science* published by GoodYearBooks. Copyright ©1994 by Hy Kim.

the sun and the earth are equal. If one is greater than the other, the one with the larger number means that the distance between the earth and the sun is longer than the other.

The number of days in each month is listed in the left column. The number of days in fall and winter is in the center column. The number of days in spring and summer is shown in the right column. The earth takes 180 days to travel from Fall Equinox to Spring Equinox.

Days of a Month		Days in Fall and/or Winter		Days of Spring & Summer	
January	31	September	8	March	10
February	28	October	31	April	30
March	31	November	30	May	31
April	30	December	31	June	30
May	31	January	31	July	31
June	30	February	28	August	31
July	31	March	21	September	22
August	31				
September	30				
October	31				
November	30				
December	31				
Total:	365	Total:	180	Total:	185

It takes 185 days to travel from Spring Equinox to Fall Equinox. Therefore, we can conclude that the earth is closer to the sun during the winter than the summer in the Northern Hemisphere. In the Southern Hemisphere, the earth is closer to the sun during the summer than the winter.

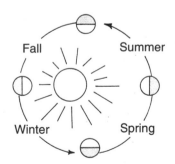

By using this data, can you settle the argument?

The earth's orbit is really elliptical, or oval, not circular. Therefore, the earth is nearer to the sun during the winter in the Northern Hemisphere.

A Latitude Finder

Longitude lines run from the North Pole to the South Pole. Latitude lines run parallel to the equator. Both types are imaginary lines that locate a place on the earth's surface.

Once a man drifted on an ocean current for four months on a piece of boat wreckage. Everybody who knew him thought he had drowned when his boat was wrecked in a storm. When he finally came home, they all gave him a sensational welcome party. He became a hero who was invited to speak on national television shows. He said that one of the survival skills he used was a latitude finder that he made with a string. You can make a latitude finder and find the latitude where you live.

For this activity, you need:

○ a piece of paper

○ a protractor

○ a ruler

○ a compass

○ a paper clip

○ string

To do this activity:

Make a hole in one corner of the paper as shown in the right-upper corner of the illustration. Using the hole as a center, draw a quarter-circle. Use a protractor to draw line segments that divide the right angle into ten degree angles as shown. Tie one end of a string to the hole and the other end to a paper clip. Your latitude finder is completed. This finder can be used at night.

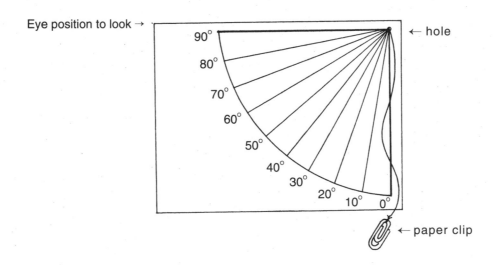

Eye position to look →

90° 80° 70° 60° 50° 40° 30° 20° 10° 0°

← hole

← paper clip

From *Showy Science* published by GoodYearBooks. Copyright ©1994 by Hy Kim.

To use the finder, locate the North Star, Polaris. A good way to find Polaris is to first locate the Big Dipper. The Big Dipper looks like a dipper. Then find the pointer stars which indicate Polaris in the constellation of the Little Dipper. Now, hold the finder and place the corner of the finder indicated as "eye position to look" to your eye. Aim the edge of the finder to Polaris. Let the paper clip hang freely. The string with the paper clip indicates the latitude of your location.

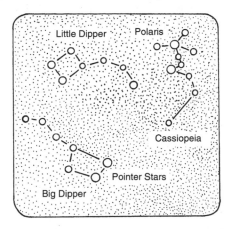

If you stand at the equator and look at the North Star with the finder, the paper clip will indicate the 0 degree line. If you stand at a 90 degree latitude spot, the North Star is directly above your head, and the paper clip will indicate the 90 degree line.

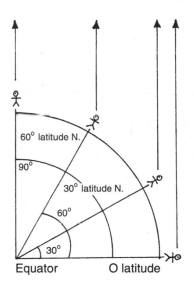

If you, like the man in the story, are drifting somewhere in the Northern Hemisphere and you have some string, you may be able to estimate your latitude. Do this by estimating the angle between the line from your eye to the North Star and the line of string suspended from your line of sight.

The Length of Day and Night

We know that one day has 24 hours. However, sometimes night is longer than day and vice versa. Some parts of the world have 24 hours of day or 24 hours of night. What makes the length of day and night differ? You can explain why the length of days and nights is different by seasons and latitude.

For this activity, you need:

- ○ a globe
- ○ a lamp

To do this activity:

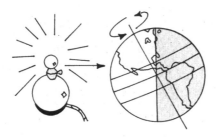

Summer Solstice

Arrange the lamp and globe at the Summer Solstice position for the Northern Hemisphere. Tilt the axis toward the sun as shown in the illustration. Turn off the lights and turn on the lamp without its lampshade. Spin the globe and watch the shadow line. If you look down from the North Pole, the shadow line looks like this:

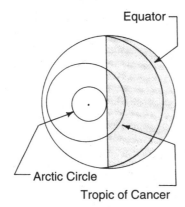

Equator

Arctic Circle

Tropic of Cancer

From *Showy Science* published by GoodYearBooks. Copyright ©1994 by Hy Kim.

The North Pole and the Arctic Circle are light all day long. If you look at the Tropic of Cancer, more than half of the circle receives daylight as shown. The shadow line will divide in half on the circle of the equator. If you visit the Arctic Circle, which is 66.5 degrees latitude north, on June 21, you will experience sunlight for 24 hours; the sun will not rise or set.

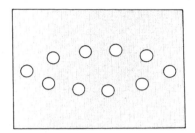

The sun will seem to travel along an ellipse as shown in the illustration. Because its rays are tilted, the sun is not as warm and bright as in the temperate weather zone.

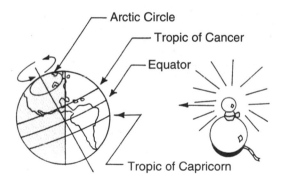

Winter Solstice

Change the globe to the Winter Solstice position so that the southern tip of the axis tilts toward the sun. Spin the globe and watch the shadow line.

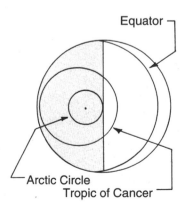

If you look down on the globe from the North Pole, the entire Arctic Circle is shadowed, which means there is no daylight at all. If you look up on the globe from the South Pole, Antarctica and the southern Arctic Circle are light. It is daytime in the South Pole and nighttime in the North Pole.

On the other hand, on the days of the Spring and Fall Equinoxes, the shadow line looks like the illustration. Every part of the world has 12 hours of daylight and 12 hours of night.

The table shows the length of daylight in the Northern Hemisphere by latitude for Summer and Winter Solstices and Spring and Fall Equinoxes.

Latitude (Degree)	Summer Solstice	Winter Solstice	Equinoxes
0	12 hr.	12 hr.	12 hr.
10	12:35	11:25	12
20	13:12	10:48	12
30	13:56	10:4	12
40	14:52	9:8	12
50	16:18	7:42	12
60	18:27	5:33	12
70	24	0	12
80	24	0	12
90	24	0	12

For example, cities located on the 40° latitude north line will have 14 hours and 52 minutes of daylight on Summer Solstice day, 9 hours and 8 minutes of daylight on Winter Solstice day, and 12 hours daylight on the Spring and Fall Equinoxes. Places on the 70° latitude north line will have two months of only daylight and two months of only night. Places on the 80° latitude north line will have four months of only daylight and only night. Places on the 90° latitude north line will have six months of only daylight and six months of only night per year. Find the latitude of your location on the globe. Estimate the length of the daylight of each season.

From *Showy Science* published by GoodYearBooks. Copyright ©1994 by Hy Kim.

Showy Science

What Causes Wind?

Did you ever think about the wind and from where it comes? Wind is moving air. These air masses are almost always moving. What is the main cause of the wind? You can make a "wind machine" and demonstrate a wind on your table. This demonstration will help you to understand why the air mass moves from high pressure areas to low pressure areas.

For this activity, you need:

- ○ an adult helper
- ○ two glass lampshades (chimneys from kerosene lamps work best)
- ○ a small cardboard box (about 10 by 15 by 25 centimeters)
- ○ a candle
- ○ a piece of clear plastic
- ○ tape
- ○ glue
- ○ a pair of scissors
- ○ a long match
- ○ a long piece of incense

To do this activity:

Stand the two lampshades on top of the box, trace the circumferences of the shades with a pencil, then cut out the two circles as shown. Now, cut a rectangular shape from the front of the box, as in the illustration. Using the glue, seal all the corners and especially the folds of the box.

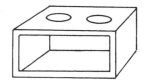

Cut out a piece of plastic to fit the front of the box and tape around the edges of the plastic as shown in the next illustration. Place a candle under one hole.

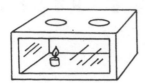

Light the candle using a long match and place the two glass lampshades in the holes as shown in the illustration.

Light a piece of incense and blow out the flame. Place the smoking end of the incense to the end of the shade under which there is no candle. Watch how the smoke moves. The smoke is drawn into the shade. The air moves from outside into the box.

Now, move the smoking end of the incense to the opening of the other shade under which the candle is burning. How does the smoke move? The smoke moves upward.

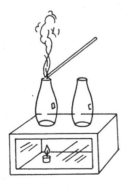

From *Showy Science* published by GoodYearBooks. Copyright ©1994 by Hy Kim.

How does this happen?

The burning candle heats the air, the heated air mass moves upward and the surrounding cooler air mass moves to where the heated air mass was. Air mass movement such as this is called a *convection current*.

Convection currents in the air are one of the major causes of wind. Some parts of the earth are warmer, such as the tropical weather zone. Other parts of the world, like the polar weather zone, are colder. Thus, convection currents occur, creating wind.

As a result of a convection current, an air mass moves from the higher pressure to the lower pressure areas. The place where the air mass is heated by the burning candle has a lower air pressure then the surrounding air mass because the hot air expands.

Land Breezes and Sea Breezes

Fishermen raise the sail on their boats in the early morning because the land breeze pushes the boat out to sea.

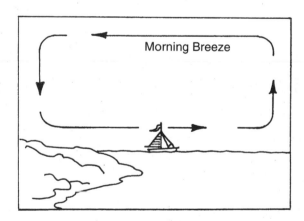

Morning Breeze

Late in the evening, fishermen raise the sail and the sea breeze pushes the boat from the sea towards the land. Long ago, fishermen used this concept of land and sea breezes to sail the seas.

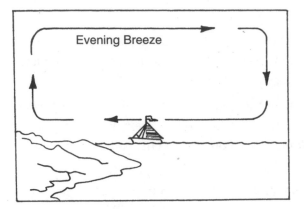

Why do we have afternoon ocean breezes (breezes moving from ocean to land) and morning land breezes (breezes moving from land to ocean)? In order to understand the reason, you can conduct a simple experiment.

For this activity, you need:

○ two containers (plastic bowls or dishes)
○ two thermometers
○ water
○ some soil

To do this activity:

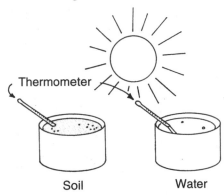

Fill one container with soil and the other container with water. Leave them in a shady spot until the temperatures of the soil and water are the same. Place a thermometer in each of the containers as shown, burying the thermometer bulb in the soil and submersing the other in the water. Place the two containers in direct sunlight and check frequently to see which one heated up more rapidly.

Which one do you think heated up quickly?

Soil heats and cools more quickly than water. Knowing this fact, we can understand how the morning land breeze and evening sea breeze come about.

From *Showy Science* published by GoodYearBooks. Copyright ©1994 by Hy Kim.

From morning to afternoon, the sun warms the land and the air above it. Meanwhile, the ocean water is still getting warm. Thus, warmer air above the land rises and cooler air above the ocean moves onto the land. On the other hand, the warmed land cools at night much more quickly than ocean water. By early morning, the ocean water is much warmer than the land. The warmer air above the water rises and cooler air from the land moves toward the ocean.

More information about global wind belts:

Oceans near the 30° north and south latitudes are usually colder than the continents at those latitudes. Air over these ocean latitudes has a higher pressure than air over the land. This difference exists through most of the year. Semi-permanent highs are found over the oceans at about 30° north and south latitudes. These are called *subtropical highs*.

Global Wind Belts

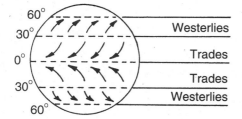

Because low pressure forms at the equator, wind blows from the subtropical highs to the low equator. These winds are called *trade winds*. The winds that move from the subtropical highs toward the poles are the *westerlies*.

A Wind Vane

The wind vane is an instrument that tells you from which direction the wind is blowing. You can make a simple wind vane.

For this activity, you need:

- ○ a drinking straw
- ○ an index card
- ○ a push pin
- ○ a pencil
- ○ a pair of scissors

To do this activity:

First, cut out a form of an arrow from the index card as shown. Split one end of the straw with scissors, insert the tail of the arrow into the split and spread glue around the joints of the arrow and the straw to hold it securely. Push a push pin through the middle of the straw into the eraser of a pencil as shown. The wind vane is completed.

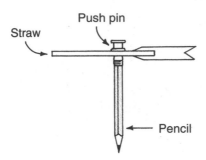

To use your wind vane, take it outside where the wind is blowing. Hold the pencil. The tail of the wind vane will indicate the direction from which the wind is blowing. To tell the direction in terms of north, south, west, east, etc., take a compass with you. Read the wind vane first, then read the compass to tell the wind direction.

A Pinwheel

A windmill is a mill used to pump water. It is operated by wind. Windmills are used on many farms. You can make a pinwheel, a miniature windmill, which will spin in a breeze.

For this activity, you need:

○ a piece of paper
○ a push pin
○ a pencil
○ a pair of scissors

From *Showy Science* published by GoodYearBooks. Copyright ©1994 by Hy Kim.

To do this activity:

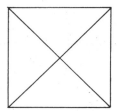

Cut the paper into a square and make diagonal creases by folding the opposite corners to the center.

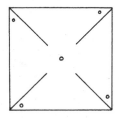

Cut along two-thirds of the creases as shown. Make small holes by pushing the pin.

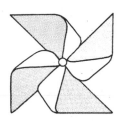 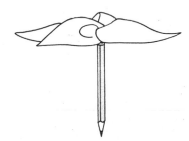

Thread the push pin through the holes of the four corners, through the center hole, then into the eraser of the pencil. The side view should look like the illustration on the right.

How does this work?

The wind turns the wheel which is connected to the vertical shaft. The turning shaft is then connected to various machines to grind grain, to pump well water, and to turn on electric generators, among other things.

ACTIVITIES FOR
EXPLORING
LIGHT

A Poster Board Saw

You can demonstrate that a poster board wheel spins like a circular power saw. It does not use electric power; it uses the power of your arm. The spinning saw will even hum as it spins. Encourage your audience to make their own poster board saw so everyone can participate in the activity.

For this activity, you need:

○ a piece of poster board or cardboard
○ a compass
○ a nail or ice pick
○ a piece of string (about 80 centimeters long)
○ a pair of scissors

To do this activity:

Use a compass (or a round object such as a cup) to trace a circle with a diameter of 5 centimeters. This measurement does not have to be exact; a circle that is a little bigger or smaller will do fine. Use a nail or an ice pick to make two small holes 1 centimeter apart in the middle of the circle.

Thread the piece of string through the holes. Tie the ends to make a loop on both sides of the wheel.

From *Showy Science* published by GoodYearBooks. Copyright ©1994 by Hy Kim.

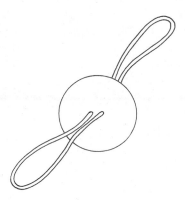

To spin the wheel, hold your hands so that your palms face each other. Bend four fingers of each hand. Insert your four bent fingers in the loop and hold the string. Whirl the wheel so that the string loop is twisted.

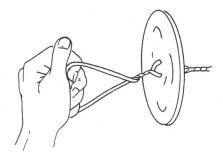

Now stretch the string with both hands so the string is tight. As the wheel spins and untwists the string, relax the string. Momentum will spin the wheel, and the string will be twisted in the other direction. When the wheel slows down, tighten the string and make the wheel spin in the other direction.

By tightening and relaxing the string, you can spin the wheel as long as you want. If you are spinning the wheel for the first time, you will probably need some practice. Many fantastic demonstrations and experiments can be done with this spinning wheel.

Color Blending With the Spinning Wheel

This demonstration shows that you can make the color white by blending yellow, blue, and red colors on a wheel. You can make the color black by blending blue, green, and red on a wheel. You will become a color blending master!

For this activity, you need:

○ the posterboard wheel you made for the previous activity
○ markers of different colors, crayons, or a watercolor set

To do this activity:

Divide one side of the wheel into three equal sections. Color each section with red, blue, and yellow. Divide the other side of the wheel into three equal sections. Color each section with red, blue, and green.

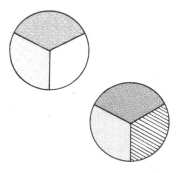

Spin the wheel by pulling the twisted string like you did in the last activity. Watch both sides of the wheel. One side is black and the other side is white!

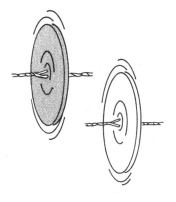

Why does this happen?

You have probably heard that artists make all different colors by mixing three primary colors. Red, green, and blue are the primary colors of light. When these primary colors are mixed, white light is produced. In this wheel experiment, these colors produced black.

Magenta, cyan, and yellow are the primary colors of pigment. When mixed together, they produce black. However, these colors produced white in this wheel experiment.

More Color Blending

You can demonstrate many color blending exercises with the same materials.

For this activity, you need:

○ the posterboard wheel you made for the previous activity
○ markers of different colors, crayons, or a watercolor set

To do this activity:

Color one side of a wheel red and blue. Color the other side red and yellow. Spin the wheel to find out what blends the colors make. One will produce purple and the other will produce orange. Try your own designs and blend new colors.

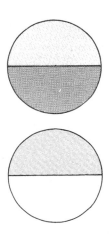

Color Illusion

Show your audience a wheel on which black stripes and black shading have been drawn. No one sees any other colors on the wheel. However, various colors appear when you spin the wheel. Even more surprisingly, you can generate different colors simply by altering the speed of the spinning wheel!

For this activity, you need:

○ a posterboard wheel (one that has a 6 to 10
    centimeter radius works best)
○ a black marker

To do this activity:

Color one-half of the wheel with black marker as shown. Use a compass to draw thin lines of semi-circles on the white part of the wheel. Use a black marker to draw arcs as in the illustration. The length of these arcs should be one-third of the semi-circles; however, you can make the length one-fourth or one-fifth. Each arc should be a different distance from the center.

Now select a well-lighted spot in the room and spin the wheel. You will see different colors appearing on the wheel! Vary the speed and observe that the red color will move outward or inward depending on the speed. You may able to see red, green, and blue.

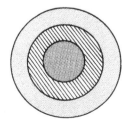

From *Showy Science* published by GoodYearBooks. Copyright ©1994 by Hy Kim.

Rolling Reader

Did you ever use a magnifying glass to read a letter, a newspaper, or a book? You can make a pop bottle magnifying glass with a empty pop bottle.

For this activity, you need:

○ an adult helper
○ a two-liter pop bottle
○ a paper towel
○ turpentine or other solvent
○ water
○ a printed page

To do this activity:

Without making a dent on the side of a two-liter pop bottle, take off its label. Have an adult help you remove the glue with a paper towel soaked in turpentine. Rinse the bottle and fill it with cold tap water. Put on the cap, making sure that no air bubbles are trapped inside the bottle. Your magnifying glass reader is ready to roll.

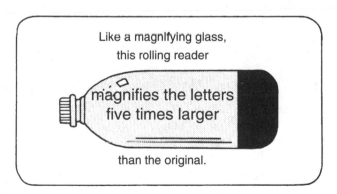

Like a magnifying glass, this rolling reader magnifies the letters five times larger than the original.

Wipe off any moisture on the outside of the bottle. Lay it on a written page and look at the written lines through the bottle. The letters will be magnified about two to ten times! As you read the material, you can simply roll the magnifier down the page.

Why does it work?

Before we find an explanation, let's do one more activity.

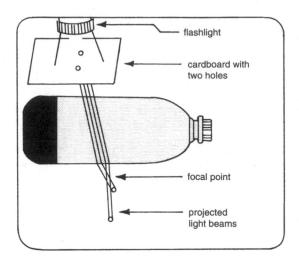

flashlight

cardboard with two holes

focal point

projected light beams

For a related activity, you need:

○ a flashlight

○ a piece of cardboard

○ a pop bottle magnifying glass

To do this activity:

Punch two holes, five centimeters apart, in the cardboard as in the illustration. Turn off the lights and close the curtains. (Evening is perfect for this activity.) Turn on the flashlight and send two beams of light through the cardboard holes and the bottle. You will see two spotlights on the wall.

Block the hole on the right side of the cardboard with your finger. Which spot of light, the right or left side, do you think will disappear? If you block the right hole, the left light spot will disappear. If you block the left hole, the right light spot will disappear. Why? Because the light beams are bent when they pass through your pop bottle magnifying glass.

As you cast the two light spots on the wall, move the system slowly toward the wall. The distance between the two light spots will get shorter. Keep moving the system until the two light spots meet. This point is called the focal point of the lens.

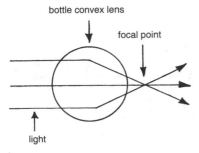

bottle convex lens

focal point

light

How does this work?

Light travels in a straight line. However, it bends when it passes from one medium to another. Light travels through a vacuum, air, water, some plastic, glass, and other transparent materials. This bending action of traveling light is called *refraction*.

Lenses that bulge outward in the middle like a magnifying glass or pop bottle lens are called convex lenses. As in the illustration of a convex pop bottle lens, bent lights meet at one point, the focal point. Some objects or letters within the focal point will look bigger. An object or a letter outside the focal point will look upside-down or reversed.

Do We Really See the Sun Before It Rises and After It Sets?

You have probably heard that we see the sun before it rises and after it sets. Yes, it is true. You can demonstrate this phenomenon with simple materials.

For this activity, you need:

- ○ a pop bottle lens
- ○ some books
- ○ a pencil
- ○ a coin

To do this activity:

Lay a pop bottle lens on a table. Stack books on both sides of the bottle as in the illustration. The heights of the two stacks must be about one centimeter higher than half the bottle when laid flat on the table.

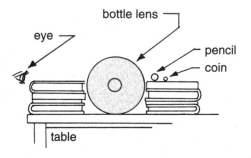

If you look down on the arrangement, it should resemble the next illustration. Place a pencil beside the bottle. Put a coin about one centimeter from the pencil as shown. Now, position your eyes at the end of the book stack. Look at the coin through the lens. Sometimes you will see two coins! Without changing your eye position, remove the lens. You can no longer see the coin because the pencil is blocking the view.

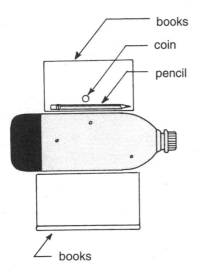

books
coin
pencil

books

What does this activity show you?

In this demonstration, the coin represents the sun; the pencil represents the horizon or a mountain; and the bottle lens represents the earth's atmosphere. When no clouds block the view in the atmosphere, we indeed see the sun before it rises and after it sets. This happens for the same reason you saw the coin through the bottle lens.

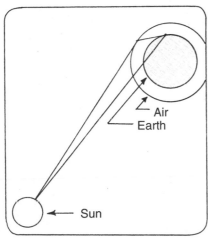

Air
Earth

Sun

The light from the sun passes through a vacuum between the sun and the earth. It then passes through the air around the earth before it reaches your eyes. The air acts like a convex lens.

A Rainbow on Your Ceiling

You can make a rainbow on your living room or classroom wall with a glass of water!

For this activity, you need:

○ a glass of water

To do this activity:

Find a spot where bright sunlight comes into the house. Fill a glass with cold water and tilt it as in the illustration. Let the light beam pass the triangular shape of the side view of water in the glass. The triangular shape of water acts as a prism. The white light beam will spread into rainbow colors as it emerges from the far side of the glass.

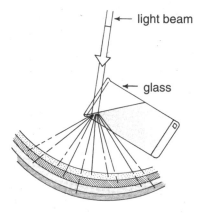

light beam

glass

An overhead projector is needed to project a rainbow on the classroom ceiling on rainy day.

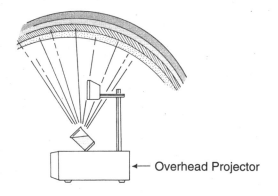

Overhead Projector

From *Showy Science* published by GoodYearBooks. Copyright ©1994 by Hy Kim.

To demonstrate the rainbow in the classroom, turn off the classroom lights. Turn on an overhead projector and place a water-glass prism on it. Now, slowly tilt the prism as in the illustration. The light band that passes through the prism will appear on the ceiling. Adjust the tilt of the glass so that blue, red, and other color bands appear in the rainbow.

For a similar activity:

Use a mirror to show a rainbow on your ceiling. Fill a container with water and place the mirror at an angle as shown in the illustration. Place the system where a beam of direct sunlight can shine on the submerged part of the mirror. A rainbow will appear on the ceiling or wall.

The light passes through the water prism as shown. It is reflected on the ceiling, making a rainbow.

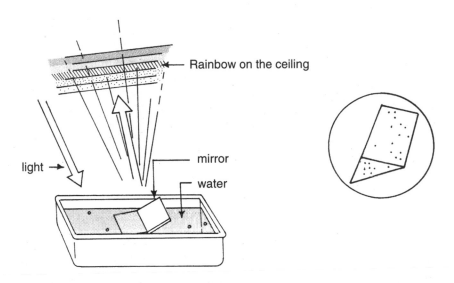

Rainbow on the ceiling

light →

mirror

water

More information about rainbows:

White light is a mixture of all the visible colors. A wedge-shaped glass prism splits white light into colors in the specific order of red, orange, yellow, green, blue, indigo, and violet. This order results because each color has a different frequency and bends differently when it is refracted. For example, red light bends least and violet light bends most in visible light.

Sometimes after rain, water drops in the sky act like prisms, splitting sunlight into many colors in the sky. As a result, we see a rainbow.

Why Is the Sky Blue?

The sky appears blue. You can demonstrate why using simple materials.

For this activity, you need:

- ◯ a pop bottle filled with water
- ◯ several drops of milk
- ◯ a flashlight

To do this activity:

Darken the room. Shine a flashlight on the pop bottle filled with water and several drops of milk as in the illustration. You will see that the milky water is bluish!

Why does the water look this way?

White light, which has all the colors in the rainbow, behaves strangely when it passes through small particles such as milky water, air with dust particles, or ocean water with many particles. The blue color bends and scatters most because of the small particles. Thus, the atmosphere, lakes, and oceans look blue because of the scattered blue color's reflection.

From *Showy Science* published by GoodYearBooks. Copyright ©1994 by Hy Kim.

Why Is the Sun Red When It Rises and Sets?

For this activity, you need:

- ○ a pop bottle filled with water
- ○ several drops of milk
- ○ a flashlight

To do this activity:

Darken the room. Shine a flashlight on a pop bottle filled with water and several drops of milk as in the illustration. If you look at the flashlight beam from the opposite side of the bottle, the light beam looks reddish like a rising or setting sun. The flashlight represents the sun; the milky water in the illustration represents the blue sky; and the reddish light represents the rising or setting sun.

Why does the water look this way?

When you look at the sun as it is rising or setting, it looks reddish because the blue color in the white light is scattered. The red is not scattered and reaches your eye.

Funny Faces by Mirrors

We use mirrors every day to see ourselves. But, did you ever see yourself with two faces or one eye? By using two mirrors, you can make yourself look like a monster.

For these activities, you need:

○ two mirrors
○ tape

To do these activities:

Place two mirrors side by side face down on a smooth surface and tape along the edges of the back side of the mirrors. The tape acts like a hinge.

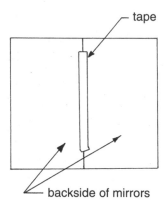

Hold the mirrors as shown in the illustration and look at your face. The two mirrors will act like just one mirror if you hold the mirrors as one piece.

Now, slowly bend the mirrors at the hinges and watch what happens to your face.

From *Showy Science* published by GoodYearBooks. Copyright ©1994 by Hy Kim.

Some part of your face will disappear in the image—perhaps your mouth, nose, or eyes! You can create many funny faces in the mirrors by moving your face and by changing the angles of the mirrors. Can you make a four-eyed face? Bend the mirrors forward at the hinges and watch the image of your face become four-eyed and two-nosed.

Hold the mirrors as shown in the illustration. You will see your normal face in the image if you hold the mirrors flat.

Now bend the mirrors at the hinge in a forward direction and watch the image of your face in the mirrors. Notice the two-faced person. Bend the mirror backward at the hinge and see the images of your face.

Activities for Exploring Light

You can make a one-eyed monster, or a no-eyed, no-mouthed, no-nosed monster. You can see the distorted images of your face better with one eye closed.

Why does it work as it does?

Each of two mirrors reflect part of your face and the separate images of your face are joined to form one whole face. In this way, some parts of your face are missing or some parts of your face are added to make the distorted image of your face.

A Money-Making Machine

Pretend that you invented a machine in which a dime is instantly changed into 10 dimes. You could be rich. By using two mirrors, you can show the images of money multiplied as many times as you wish.

For this activity, you need:

❍ two rectangular mirrors
❍ tape

To do this activity:

Place two mirrors together face to face and tape one side as shown in the illustration. As in the previous activity, the tape will act like a hinge.

From *Showy Science* published by GoodYearBooks. Copyright ©1994 by Hy Kim.

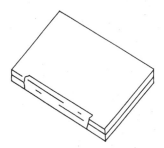

Open the mirrors and place a coin in front of the mirrors as shown. The mirrors refract one image of the coin so that you see two coins, one real and the other the image.

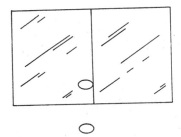

Now, slightly close the mirrors at the angle of the hinge and observe the number of coins. You can make three coins as you close the mirrors.

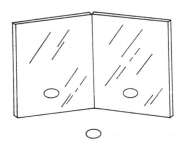

You can make four coins, and continue to make coins, by narrowing the angles between two mirrors. What is the maximum number of coins can you make?

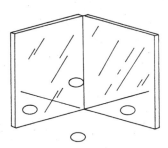

By adding one more mirror to the two mirrors as shown in the next illustration, you can see many coins.

Activities for Exploring Light

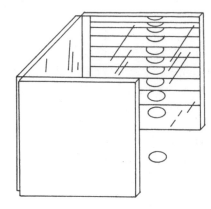

Draw a picture on a piece of paper. Look at the picture through the hinged mirrors. The many images of your drawing make totally strange configurations.

On a piece of paper, draw lines as shown in the illustration. Slide the two hinged mirrors from the lower line to the upper line. What shapes are formed in the mirrors?

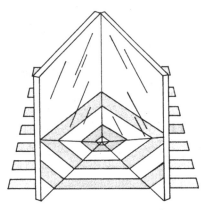

You can make a pentagon, a square, or any other polygons!

From *Showy Science* published by GoodYearBooks. Copyright ©1994 by Hy Kim.

Polygons and Angles With Mirrors

Many-sided figures, such as the triangle and square, are called polygons. Polygons that have equal-length sides and equal angles are called regular polygons. For example, a triangle that has equal sides and equal angles is called a regular triangle. You can make make regular polygons with the two hinged mirrors.

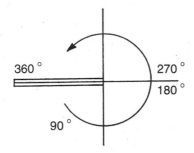

One right angle measures 90° on a protractor. Two right angles measure 180°; three right angles measure 270°; and four right angles measure 360°. A protractor is an instrument with which we can measure the angles. However, since one complete rotation is 360°, you can use the two hinged mirrors to find out the angles.

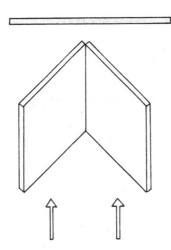

For this activity, you need:
- ○ two hinged mirrors
- ○ a pen or pencil
- ○ a piece of paper

Draw a solid line on a piece of paper and slide the two hinged mirrors as shown.

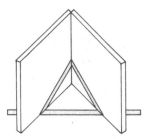

Adjust the mirrors so that a triangle is formed, as in the illustration. Look at the triangle.

At the center of the triangle you can see three line segments that divide the 360° angles. Each division of angle must be 120°. The two mirrors are standing on 120° angles. By this method, you can make polygons as well as find angles.

No. of Sides of Polygons		Size of Mirror Angle
3	Triangle	120°
4	Quadrilateral	
5	Pentagon	
6	Hexagon	
7	Heptagon	
8	Octagon	
9	Nonagon	
10	Decagon	
12	Dodecagon	

Make a four-sided figure, a quadrilateral, and calculate the mirror's angle. If you adjust the mirrors to make a quadrilateral, the shape will be square. Because there are four divisions in the center of the square, 360° divided by four will make 90°. By closing the angles of the mirror you can create all the listed polygons and calculate the angles. You can also use a calculator to compute the angles.

From *Showy Science* published by GoodYearBooks. Copyright ©1994 by Hy Kim.

Mirror-Image Puzzles

For this activity, you need:

○ two mirrors, hinged with tape on the back
○ paper
○ a pencil

To do this activity:

Write a "T" on the paper and place this on a table top. Stand the hinged mirrors behind the "T" and facing you, as shown in the illustration below.

How do the images appear? On another piece of paper, make a copy of the images. The images and the the letter T should look like the illustration below.

Can you detect the correct illustration among the three following illustrations?

From *Showy Science* published by GoodYearBooks. Copyright ©1994 by Hy Kim.

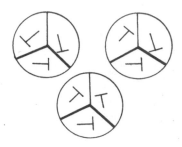

Which one is the correct one? If you are not sure, place the hinged mirrors on the thicker lines and look at the images again. The upper right illustration is the correct one. Make a puzzle of your own by using the three frames.

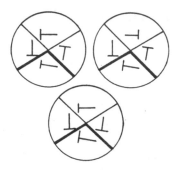

Now we will use four-frame puzzles. First, without using the mirrors, figure out the correct illustration. Then verify your answer with the mirrors.

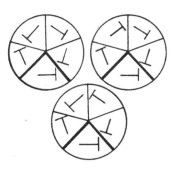

This is a five-frame puzzle. Can you detect the correct illustration without using the mirrors?

From *Showy Science* published by GoodYearBooks. Copyright ©1994 by Hy Kim.

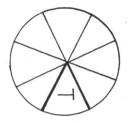

Draw the images for each frame and check the illustration by placing the mirrors on the thicker black lines.

A Periscope

A periscope is an instrument by which you can view an area without being seen. Pretend you are spying on somebody who is behind a wall. You are able to raise a periscope and observe him or her without exposing yourself. It is possible to make a simple periscope.

For this activity, you need:

○ an adult helper

○ two half-gallon cardboard milk cartons

○ two small mirrors

○ a piece of cardboard

○ tape

○ glue

○ a pair of scissors

○ a knife

To do this activity:

Cut off the tops of both cartons. Cut a square measuring 9 by 9 centimeters at the bottom of each of the two cartons as shown.

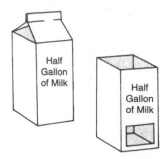

Cut out a piece of cardboard 9 by 30.7 centimeters. Fold the cardboard into a right triangle with the dimensions of 9 by 9 by 12.7 centimeters. Tape the joint of the triangle. Tape or glue a small mirror on the face of the 9 by 12.7 cm side of the cardboard. (A 9 by 12 cm mirror is ideal but a smaller one works too.)

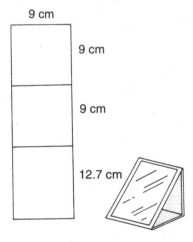

Now make another triangular mirror mount. Glue the triangular cardboard inside the milk carton so that the mirror shows through the opening. Repeat the same procedure in the second carton.

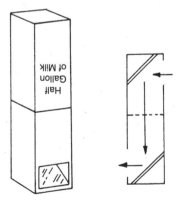

Now, place one carton over another top to top and tape them together as shown. Be sure the mirrors of the top and bottom cartons are on opposite sides of each other. Your periscope is ready to use. Hide yourself under a window sill, raise the periscope, and watch outside. Nobody outside can see you, but you can see them!

From *Showy Science* published by GoodYearBooks. Copyright ©1994 by Hy Kim.

A

Action & reaction, 228

Aerodynamic
> pendulum, 210
> string, 211

Air
> expansion and contraction, 4
> molecules, 3
> pressure, 25
> taking up space, 8

Airplane, paper, 242

Algae, 106, 108

Altimeter, 27

Anaerobic, 181

Angles with mirrors, 297

Aquarium
> bottle, 104
> snail, 108

Arctic circle, 267

Atomizer, 48

Auxins, 139

Axis, tilt of, 257

B

Bacilli, 193

Bacteria, 192

Balancing
> a fork & spoon, 205
> a ruler, 206

Balloon
> rocket, 231
> hot air, 57
> hovering, 46

Barometer, 24, 26

Bean
> plant, 139
> sprout, 147

Bernoulli's principle, 43

Boiling point
> of alcohol, 183
> of water, 183

Bottle
> musical instrument, 51
> planter, 132
> thermometer, 21

Bottle rocket, 224
> engine, 224
> trigger, 226
> water engine, 225

C

Capillary action, 90

Carbon dioxide gas, 171

Chlorophyll, 95

Chromatogram, 93

Clay boat, 246

Cloud machine, 231

Cohesion, 73

Cohesive force, 68

Color
> bands, 92
> blending, 280
> illusion, 282

Community chart, 198

Consumer
> first level, 198
> second level, 198
> third level, 198

Convection current, 85

Convex lens, 285

Crushing pop cans, 18

Cotyledon, 136

Cytoplasm, 197

D

Dancing penny, 4
Day and night, length of, 266
Decomposers, 170
Diaphragm, 33
Dicotyledon, 136
Distance between sun & earth, 262
Duckweed, 109

E

Ear model, 54
        inner ear, 56
        outer ear, 56
Earth's rotation, 257
Egg, swelling and shrinking, 129
Eggshell, peeling of, 126
Ellipse, 267
Embryo, 136
Epicotyle, 136
Equinox, 261
Estimating cargo, 252
Eutrophication, 114

F

Fermentation, 181
Fish
        and green plants, 114
        in cold water, 115
Floating and sinking
        egg, 78
        soft drink, 81
Floating
        clay boat, 250
        pins, 75
Focal point, 284
Food, salting of, 196

Foucault pendulum, 212
Freezing point of water, 100
Friction, 215
Friction efficent car, 216
Funny faces using mirrors, 292

G

Geotropism, 141
Geranium, 154
Germ theory, 194
Gravity, 201
        center of, 204
Gravity-powered race car, 216
Greenhouse, bag, 140
Growing new plants
        African violet, 157
        coleus, 152
        from an offset, 161
        from bulbs, 167
        from cuttings, 152
        Peperomia, 158
        rex begonia, 160
        spider, 161
        sweet potato, 162
        wandering Jew, 152

H

Helicopter, 239, 241
Hydrometer, 79
Hydroponics, 167
Hyphae, 189

From *Showy Science* published by GoodYearBooks. Copyright ©1994 by Hy Kim.

I

Ice cream shake-up, 99
Ice
> cube, 101
> power, 98
> puzzle, 100

Ichthyophthrius, 112
Inertia, 215
Inhale and exhale, 31

L

Land breeze, 270
Latitude finder, 264
Life cycle
> mealworm, 124
> monarch, 118
> mosquito, 120

Lifting a canning jar, 15
Lung model, 31

M

Marble game, 213
Mason jar magic, 16
Mealworm farm, 123
Metamorphosis, 118, 124
Milkweed, 117
Mold
> blue-green, 190
> bread, 185
> common, 188

Molting, 118
Monarch butterfly, 116
Money making machine, 294
Monocotyledon, 136

Moon
> orbit of, 234
> model of, 234
> phases of, 235

Mosquito
> aquarium, 119
> fish, 112
> larvae, 120

Mucor, 188
Mucus, 195

O

Obedient diver, 70
Osmosis, 197
Oxidation, 39
Oxygen bubbles, 36

P

Pendulum, 208
Penicillium, 192
Penny barge, 252
Period, 209
Periscope, 301
Photosynthesis, 144, 173
Phototropism, 139
Pigment
> in green leaves, 94
> primary colors of, 93

Pinwheel, 274
Plant digestion, 136
Planter, bottle, 132
Plants
> auto-watering system, 150
> breathing, 34
> grown from bulbs, 167
> number in a pot, 146
> potato, 162, 165
> self-watering system, 149

Polaris, 265
Polygons by mirrors, 297
Pond water, 106
Poster board saw, 278
Primary colors, 281
Primary root, 135
Prisms, 288
Propeller, 239
Puzzle, mirror image, 299

R

Rainbow on ceiling, 288
Refraction, 285
Rolling coffee can, 222
Rolling reader, 283
Rusting steel-wool, 39

S

Salt crystals, 96
Seasons, 259
Seat belt, 219
Seed sprouting conditions, 144
Siphon, 87
Sky, blue, 290
Smoking machine, 87
Snail
    aquarium, 108
    dormant stage, 109
Solid expanded by heat, 40
Solstice, 260
Spirilli, 193
Spore, 189
Sprouting seeds and carbon dioxide, 138
Square puzzle, 244
Standing apple, 207
Stomata, 156

Sugar
    in soft drink, 82
    to alcohol, 184
Sunset, red, 291
Surface tension, 76

T

Terminal bud, 155
Thigmotropism, 142
Tornado machine, 28
Trigger, bottle rocket, 226
Tropic of Cancer, 259
Tropic of Capricorn, 259
Turbinates, 195

V

Vacuum, partial, 13
Volume of clay, 246

W

Water
    clock, 91
    dropping contest, 73
    engine, 229
    evaporation contest, 156
    hourglass, 86
    jet puzzle, 65
    pond, 106
    self-refilling bowl of pets, 63
    spout, 19
    trick, 62
Whistle, 50, 52
Wind vane, 273

Y

Yeast,
    conditions of growth, 176
    rotting banana, 170

Annotated Bibliography

Activities for Exploring Air

Branley, Franklyn M. *Air Is All Around You; Volcanoes; Oxygen Keeps You Alive.* HarperCollins. The above titles are from the Let's Read and Find Out series. These books contain information designed to be used as an introduction to the title subject. Drawings, maps, and diagrams are included to reinforce the text that contains basic facts about each subject.

Gibbons, Gail. *Weather Forecasting.* Aladdin, 1993. A look at a weather station and the equipment needed to track, gauge and predict the weather.

Gibbons, Gail. *Weather Words and What They Mean.* Holiday. A dictionary of words pertaining to the study of weather and definitions of each word. A short explanation follows each entry.

Johnson, Neil. *Fire and Silk: Flying in a Hot Air Balloon.* Little, 1991. The principles of operating a hot-air balloon are explained clearly. Includes text illustrated with photographs of the journey.

Lauber, Patricia. *Volcano: The Eruption and Healing of Mt. St. Helens.* Bradbury Press, 1986. Describes the destruction caused by Mt. St. Helens, what caused its eruption, and the aftermath of the event. Photographs illustrate the informative text.

Available in paperback and trade edition. Winner of the Newberry Honor Award.

Scullard, Sue. *The Great Around the World Balloon Race.* Dutton, 1991. A picture book showing contestants from around the world guiding their brilliantly colored balloons on a race around the world.

Simon, Seymour. *Soap Bubble Magic.* Lothrop, 1985. Experiments using soap and air to make bubbles.

Simon, Seymour. *Volcanoes.* Morrow, 1988. Twenty-five color photos accompany concise text that explains the creation of and the effects of tornadoes.

Smith, Henry. *Amazing Air;* A Science Club Series book. Lothrop, 1983. This book examines the characteristics of air, water in air, air pressure, and more. (Experiments include safety instructions and glossary.)

Volcano and Earthquake; Eyewitness Books. Random House. The style of this series makes the study of science appealing and inviting. Facts are trustworthy and illustrations and photographs jump from the pages.

Zubrowski, Bernie. *Balloons: Building and Experimenting With Inflatable Toys.* Morrow, 1990. This Boston Children's Museum Book is an introduction to the physical properties of gasses and the scientific concepts of force and pressure.

Activities for Exploring Water

Doubilet, Anne. *Under the Sea From A to Z.* Crown, 1991. A sentence of large bold print gives one fact on each page for younger readers and a paragraph in smaller print that contains expanded information for older readers. Color photographs accompany text.

Ehlert, Lois. *Red Leaf, Yellow Leaf.* Harcourt Brace Jovanovich, 1991. Brilliant colors and creative projects explain the process of changing color in the maple leaf. A picture book.

Hunter, Mollie. *Mermaid Summer.* HarperCollins, 1988. A novel about the grandchildren of a fisherman who try to discover the reason men and ships are disappearing off the coast of Scotland. Local legends imply a mermaid directs the strong currents that are responsible for those lost at sea.

Johnson, Sylvia A. *How Leaves Change.* First Avenue Editions, 1986. Succinct text explains the process of color change in leaves. Color photos and diagrams help present facts and enliven the book.

Jonas, Ann. *Color Dance.* Greenwillow, 1989. This picture book features three dancers waving scarves of primary colors. As they dance through the pages, the overlapping scarves create new colors. Simple text and drawings but the concept of mixing colors may inspire experimentation with paints and other materials.

Seed, Deborah. *Water Science.* Addison-Wesley, 1992. Contains water projects and information about water. Includes information about water in the body, what water is and what it can do, water in the world, shortages and pollution, and water games and tricks.

The Crystal Kit. Running Press. An activity kit and book that explains the process of creating crystals and directions to create them.

Watson, Philip. *Liquid Magic*; A Science Club Series book. Morrow, 1993. An introduction to the properties of liquids. Experiments with motion, density, enzymes and crystals are included. (Contains safety instructions and glossary.)

Weiss, Harvey. *Submarines and Other Underwater Craft.* HarperCollins, 1990. Included are illustrated facts about the history of submarines, how they work, and their uses and design.

Activities for Exploring Animals

Amazing Beetles; Amazing Butterflies and Moths; Amazing Fish; Eyewitness Juniors. Dorling Kindersley. Random House. These simplified versions of the Eyewitness books provide information, photos, and diagrams for the younger reader.

Demi. *Demi's Secret Garden*. Henry Holt. This collection of poems about insects is vividly illustrated with innovative and highly decorative drawings of the subject of each poem. Suitable for all ages. Especially effective to motivate art projects and promote an appreciation of poetry at the junior high level.

George, Jean Craighead. *The Moon of the Monarch Butterflies*. HarperCollins, 1993. A special story that describes the journey of a monarch butterfly as she leaves Mexico and migrates north to Ontario.

Gibbons, Gail. *The Monarch Butterfly*. Holiday, 1989. Facts and drawings explain the butterfly's metamorphosis, identify characteristics of each stage of development, its habitat, migration and much more in this well designed and informative publication. Author's work is always well researched.

Goor, Ron, and Goor, Nancy. *Insect Metamorphosis: From Egg to Adult*. Atheneum, 1990. A straightforward look at the amazing process that produces insects of all sorts.

Mudd, Maria. *The Beetle*; illustrated by Wendy Smith-Griswold. Stewart Tabori Chang. An intricate pop-up book that enlarges the beetle to many times its life size and presents fascinating facts about its life.

Pond and River; Insect; Eyewitness Books. Random House. Large format design of this series provides good balance between illustrations and text. Whether they look just at the photos and diagrams or read the text, children will learn effortlessly from these books.

Rood, Ronald. *Tide Pools*. HarperCollins. A slim volume that contains extensive information about creatures found in the small pools at the seashore. Snails, crabs, sea lettuce, jellyfish, and starfish arc some of the sea dwellers examined.

Schwartz, David M. *The Hidden Life of the Pond*; photographs by Dwight Kuhn. Crown, 1988. Color photographs dominate the pages full of clear and concise text.

Stidworthy, John. *Ponds and Streams*. Troll, 1990. A thin but informative book that looks at water, microscopic water life, breathing in water, and hidden intricate creatures found in pond and streams.

Tide Pool; Swamp Life; Pond Life; Look Closer series. Dorling Kindersley. The series is published for young readers but the clear presentation of the material makes them valuable additions to the collection of science materials at the intermediate level.

Wu, Norbert. *Fish Faces*. Henry Holt, 1993. A look at the faces and other body parts of fish found in the sea and in aquariums. Striking color and attractive layout make this book appealing to students at various levels and is an excellent model for art projects.

Activities for Exploring Plants

Lauber, Patricia. *Seeds: Pop Stick Glide*; photographs by Jerome Wexller. Crown, 1988. Well organized book book that uses crisp black and white photos. Written by a recognized children's science writer.

Meltzer, Milton. *The Amazing Potato: A Story in Which the Incas, Conquistadors, Marie Antoinette, Thomas Jefferson, Wars, Famines, and French Fries All Play a Part*. HarperCollins, 1992. Relates the humble potato to a great many events and celebrates the versatility of this vegetable, a staple at the table and the basis for many experiments.

Plant; Eyewitness Books. Dorling Kindersley. Random House. Large format design of this series provides good balance between illustrations and text. Whether they look just at the photos and diagrams or read the text, children will learn effortlessly using these books.

The Visual Dictionary of Plants. Dorling Kindersley. Includes a wide array of plants presented as a whole, then taken apart and examined. Parts of the plants are labeled and pictured close-up in color photos. Classifications, photosynthesis, germination, and reproduction are but a few of the chapter headings. Text and illustrations in books by this publisher are comprehensive sources to use in the science curriculum.

Activities for Exploring Microbes

Berger, Melvin. *Germs Make Me Sick*; Let's Read and Find Out. HarperCollins, 1985. The Let's Read and Find Out series contains uncomplicated text and simple but straightforward drawings and illustrations. The format is designed to establish basic understanding of the subject indicated in the title. Grade 3.

Grillone, Lisa, and Gennaro, Joseph. *Small Worlds Close Up*. Crown. Minute surface details of a variety of objects, plants, insects, and animals through the lens of a microscope.

Kumin, Maxine. *The Microscope*; illustrated by Arnold Lobel. HarperCollins, 1984. An illustrated poem in one volume that introduces the scientist Leeuwenhoek to young readers and speaks about his accomplishments and the tiny creatures he studied.

Seixas, Judith S. *Alcohol - What It Is, What It Does*. Morrow, 1977. Alcohol facts presented in big print and sparse text.

Stwertka, Eve, and Stwerka, Albert. *Cleaning Up - How Trash Becomes Treasure*. Messner Publishers. Includes chapters with information about decomposition of trash and what happens when bacteria decays.

White, Ryan, and Cunningham, Ann Marie. *Ryan White, My Own Story*. Dial, 1991. This is the poignant and powerful story of a victim of AIDS .The victorious spirit of Ryan White is especially moving for young adult readers

Activities for Exploring Gravity, Motion, and Other Forces

Ardley, Neil. *The Science Book of Gravity*; *The Science Book of Motion*. Harcourt Brace Jovanovich, 1992. Experiments using basic principles of the forces. Each step is illustrated with color photos.

Branley, Franklyn M. *Rockets and Satellites*; Let's Read and Find Out. HarperCollins, 1987. The reading level for this book is appropriate for third grade students at the top level. All books in this series contain information designed to be used as an introduction to the titles topic. Drawings, maps, and diagrams are included to reinforce the text that contains basic facts about each subject.

Force; Motion; Flying Machine; Eyewitness Books. Dorling Kindersley, Random House. Large format design of this series provides a good balance between illustrations and text. Whether they just look at the photos and diagrams or read the text, children will learn effortlessly from these books.

Freedman, Russell. *Wright Brothers: How They Invented the Airplane*. Holiday, 1991. A well-researched photo biography by a dependable and award winning historian/author.

Hortelius, Margaret. *Zoom: The Complete Paper Airplane Kit*. Putnam, 1991. Instructions for making paper airplanes. Paper included.

Janice VanCleave's Gravity; Spectacular Science Projects. Wiley. Experiments designed to be used for science fair projects.

Lindbergh, Reeve. *View from the Air: Charles Lindberg's Earth & Sky*. Viking, 1992. The daughter of the famous aviator documents the last flights of her father over the landscape of New England.

Macaulay, David. *The Way Things Work*. Houghton Mifflin, 1988. The definitive encyclopedia that offers comprehensive information about a wide variety of mechanical objects presented in an accessible format with concise text and illuminating illustrations.

Siebert, Diane. *Plane Song*; illustrated by Wendell Minor. HarperCollins, 1993. A lyrical poem expresses the exhilaration and majesty of flight. Realistic paintings of planes aloft enhance the text.

Simon, Seymour. *The Paper Airplane Book*; illustrated by Byron Barton. Viking, 1971. Directions for creating paper airplanes. Include principles of flight and aircraft design.

Thirteen Moons on Turtle's Back: A Native American Year of Moons. Retold by Bruchas, Joseph, and London, Jonathan; illustrated by Thomas Locker. Putnam, 1992. Phases of the moon are explained according to legends from various Indian tribes. A picture book with full color, lyrical, paintings that illustrate the text.

Tompert, Ann. *Grandfather Tang's Story*. Crown, 1990. An old man tells a story to his young niece using tanagrams. As the story progresses, the pieces are re-arranged.

Watson, Philip. *Super Motion*; A Science Club Series book. Lothrop, 1983. Simple science experiments explore motion, balance, magnetism and more. Safety instructions and glossary included.

Activities for Exploring Earth

Baker, Wendy, and Haslam, Andrew. *Make It Work! Earth: A Creative, Hands-On Approach to Science*; photographs by Jon Baines. Macmillan. Models and instructions for creating experiments and interpreting data guide the young scientist and help him/her develop scientific thinking about the planet Earth.

Branley, Franklyn. *What Makes Day and Night; Sunshine Makes the Seasons; The Moon Seems to Change; Eclipse: Darkness in Daytime*; Let's Read and Find Out series. HarperCollins. The reading level for this series is appropriate for third grade students at the top level. All books contain information designed to be used as an introduction to the title topic. Drawings, maps, and diagrams are included to reinforce the text that contains basic facts about each subject.

Ekoomiak, Normee. *Arctic Memories*. Henry Holt, 1990. The text in the English and Inuit language presents customs and traditions of the region.

Parker, Steve. *The Earth and How It Works*; See and Explore Library. Dorling Kindersley, 1993. Drawings and diagrams illustrate the earth's components.

Simon, Seymour. *The Sun*. Morrow, 1986. Comprehensive text and impressive photographs document this exploration of the sun. Author's works are always well researched and trustworthy.

Activities for Exploring Light

Anno, Mitsumasa. *Shadowland*. Orchard. This book, which shows the parallel worlds of fantasy and realism, features the land of shadows portrayed in dramatic oriental paper cuts.

Ardley, Neil. *The Science Book of Light*. Harcourt Brace Jovanovich, 1991. Simple experiments for exploring concepts of light. Each step is illustrated with color photos.

Demi. *Demi's Reflective Fables*. Putnam, 1988. A square of silver reflecting paper included in the book interprets the fables when rolled into a cylinder and placed on the page. A picture book with appeal for various ages.

Gibbons, Gail. *Beacons of Light: Lighthouses*. Morrow, 1990. The history of lighthouses and the modern equipment used today to guide the men and ships at sea.

Light; Eyewitness Science series. Dorling Kindersley. Explores the world of light. Includes the concepts of reflection, shadow, color, electromagnetic spectrum and more. Spectacular photos.

Watson, Philip. *Light Fantastic*. Lothrop, 1983. The properties of light are explored, including reflection, color optical illusions and more. Safety instructions and glossary included.

Zubrowski, Bernie. *Mirrors: Finding Out about the Properties of Light*. Morrow. This Boston Children's Museum Book contains experiments exploring the many uses of light in creating illusions, games, and machines.